MOSCOW REVEALED

Katy Benton Murrell

ALSO BY JOHN FREEMAN

LONDON REVEALED

A GUIDE TO PHOTOGRAPHING CHILDREN

BRITAIN · LONDON · IRELAND

THE COASTS OF BRITAIN

THE PHOTOGRAPHER'S HANDBOOK

ALSO BY KATHLEEN BERTON

MOSCOW: AN ARCHITECTURAL HISTORY

MOSCOW REVEALED

JOHN FREEMAN

WITH TEXT BY
KATHLEEN BERTON

Doubleday

LONDON · NEW YORK · TORONTO · SYDNEY · AUCKLAND

TRANSWORLD PUBLISHERS LTD
61-63 Uxbridge Road, London W5 5SA

TRANSWORLD PUBLISHERS (AUSTRALIA) PTY LTD
15-23 Helles Avenue, Moorebank, NSW 2170

TRANSWORLD PUBLISHERS (NZ) LTD
Cnr Moselle and Waipareira Aves,
Henderson, Auckland

DOUBLEDAY CANADA LTD
105 Bond Street, Toronto, Ontario M5B 1Y3

Published 1991 by Doubleday
a division of Transworld Publishers Ltd

Copyright © Photographs John Freeman 1991
Text Kathleen Berton 1991
Designed by Peter Campbell

The right of John Freeman and Kathleen Berton to be identified
as the authors of this work has been asserted in accordance
with sections 77 and 78 of the Copyright Designs and Patents
Act 1988.

A CIP Catalogue record for this title is available
from the British Library.
0–385–40123–X

Illustrations on title pages: *21A and B: Kuskovo: the grotto
decorated with shell designs completed in 1771.*

Typeset by Falcon Graphic Art Ltd,
Wallington, Surrey
Printed and bound in Great Britain by
Butler & Tanner Ltd, Frome and London

For my children Katie and Luke
John Freeman

For my children Sarah, Tim, Kate and Alice
Kathleen Berton

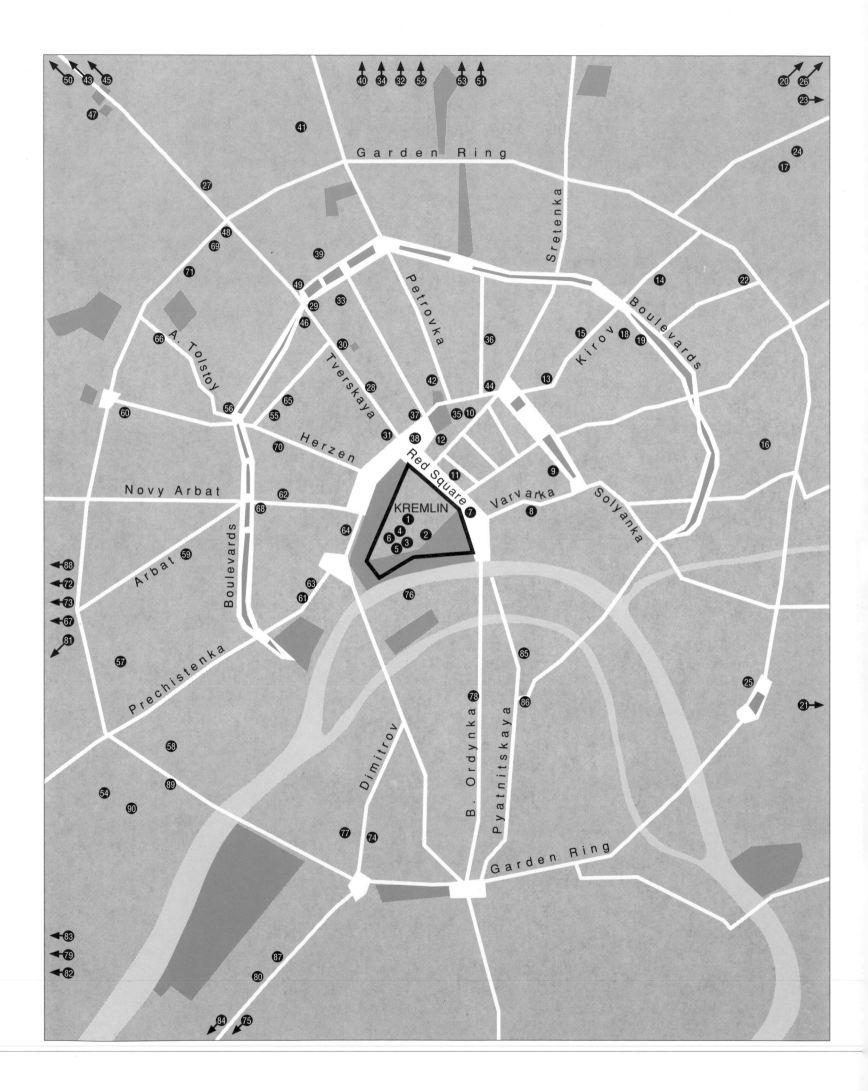

CONTENTS

ACKNOWLEDGEMENTS

A book such as *Moscow Revealed* owes its realization to many people. In particular many thanks go to Sally Gaminara, editorial director of Doubleday, who grasped the idea and saw it through from an outline to the book before you while giving birth to a son along the way. To Broo Doherty for her unfailing enthusiasm and care in editing the text, and to Peter Campbell for his diligence over the design.

John Freeman would like to say a special thank you to Octavia Hedley-Dent, his assistant throughout the months of shooting in Moscow, for her geniality and dedication that made life tolerable in sometimes difficult circumstances. And to Sue Sharpe for her whole hearted support, who liaised between London and Moscow, ensuring the smooth processing of film and the supply of such goodies as chocolate oranges.

Kathleen Berton is deeply grateful to her patient spouse, Geoffrey Murrell, whose sage advice, based on long experience of the Soviet Union, was always illuminating and whose grasp in her absence of household duties was unexpectedly sure.

Perhaps more than most undertakings, *Moscow Revealed* could not have been accomplished without the generosity of Russian and English friends living in the Soviet Union who provided unstinting assistance. Their constant and generous support and hospitality at a time of severe shortages was also a major factor in smoothing the path over the months it took to complete the photography. We are particularly grateful to Kate Cook-Horujy whose expertise, energy and boundless enthusiasm were always at our disposal and whose assistance and ingenious suggestions did much to make the project a success. The distinguished and good-humoured Moscow historian, Sergei Romanyuk, gave us invaluable advice and proved more than once to be an able photographic assistant. His wife, Galina, in addition to lavish hospitality, proved adept at finding solutions to tricky problems. Vera Nanivskaya, with her husband, Valery Ivanov, gave freely of their time and provided vital administrative assistance while receiving an endless procession of other visitors. Anton and Toma Lavrentiev generously offered much needed accommodation while their children, Dasha and Tima, together with other friends, entertained us with charm, wit and song. We are also grateful for accommodation provided by Galina Kemarskaya and her family. Invaluable support, time and advice were given by the British Ambassador and his wife, Sir Rodric and Lady Braithwaite. Terry and Grace Garrett, Terry Sandell, Ian Davies, Bridget Flavell, Carmel Power and other members of the British Embassy were also unfailingly kind and always ready to give help and make suggestions.

Assistance was also liberally extended by the Australian, French, Greek and Italian Embassies. We would like to mention the kindness of the curators at the Ostankino and Kuskovo palaces who allowed us to photograph the museums when they were closed to the public. The charm of the Tolstoy Museum was enhanced by the kindness of the director, Maxim Gorokhov. The splendours of the Aleksei Morozov Mansion were revealed to us by the talented architect-restorer, Natalya Safontseva. The architect, Leonid Nenaglyadkin, of the superbly restored Metropole Hotel infected us with his enthusiasm.

The authorities of the many churches we approached were unfailingly co-operative in finding a time when we could photograph – not easy in the conditions of the religious revival and increasing demand for baptisms and marriages in addition to the normal services.

A special thank you goes to Helen Womack and her husband, Kostya Gagarin, Irina Gubinet, Lisa Tucker, and Ruth and Jonathan Steele. We are also grateful for the co-operation and help of Alexander Bulgakov, Lidia Bykovtseva, Mikhail Byshkov, Alexander Chernayaev, Vladimir Dankov, Vladlen Davydov, Ulyana Dmitrievna, Vladimir Dlugach, Lt.-Col. Mikhail Globenko, Tatiana Khinkhis, Konstantin Levykin, Yelena Lukicheva, Alexander Meshchersky, Lev and Rika Razgon, Anatoly Sedolets, Galina Shchutskaya, Victor Smorodsky, Vladimir Tikhonov, Arkady Vaksberg, Mark Zakharov, Volodya Zakharov, Boris Zazersky, and the collective at the Theatre of History.

Finally, we were most heartened by the warmth and kindness of all the other friends together with the artists, musicians, writers and philosophers who appear in *Moscow Revealed*. To all these people and to the many helpful and friendly Muscovites we encountered along the way, we would like to express our heartfelt thanks.

John Freeman would like to thank the following organizations for their assistance and support with the photography for *Moscow Revealed*:

KODAK PROFESSIONAL PHOTOGRAPHY DIVISION for supplying Kodak Ektachrome film

LEEDS PHOTOVISUAL LIMITED for supplying professional photographic equipment

POLAROID (UK) LIMITED for supplying Polaroid film

PUSH ONE (CHELSEA) LIMITED for all E6 processing

THE STUDIO WORKSHOP LIMITED for supplying Sinar cameras and Broncolor lighting

INTRODUCTION

Moscow is a strangely exciting city. Superficially, it appears forbidding, its main avenues lined with uninviting, monumental blocks of cold official buildings giving off the unmistakable smell of the totalitarian bleakness of the Stalin and post-Stalin era. Visiting foreigners can feel alienated at first, aware of watching eyes, of unsmiling, indifferent faces. Yet, although initially Moscow seems to hide its character, on better acquaintance it opens up to reveal a warm, hospitable, somewhat bizarre nature.

The city has survived remarkably well considering its turbulent history. Even more astonishing, its interiors of pre-Revolutionary buildings are still virtually intact seventy years after plans for the communist model city were announced. One explanation for this may be the painfully slow pace of Russian redevelopment; plans made fifty years ago are only now being considered. Whatever the reasons, the interiors of Moscow's buildings were virtually unknown during the closed period of Stalin, Khrushchev and Brezhnev. With the changes in the political climate, the new policies of *perestroika* and *glasnost* under Gorbachev have begun to wear down the traditional secretiveness of Russian society, and a more open and accessible relationship with the Soviet public is rapidly coming about. Thus our quest to discover the unexplored interiors of Moscow's amazing architecture would have been impossible only a few years ago. Even if viewing some of the interiors might have been allowed, permission to photograph would have been most unlikely. *Glasnost*, in such a short space of time, has truly revolutionized Russian attitudes. Even the military academies have opened their doors.

Moscow's singular architectural history requires some explanation. Now a city of at least 9 million people, it was the capital of Russia from the fourteenth until the early eighteenth century when Peter the Great removed his capital to the swamps of the Neva estuary in one fell swoop. Moscow retained an aura of former greatness, however, continuing to act as a kind of second capital, where the emperors and empresses celebrated their coronations, where the nobility kept large houses and where commerce played a vital role. Moscow never entirely lost its preeminence to St Petersburg and when, in 1918, the Bolsheviks, under threat of imminent German invasion, moved the capital back to the ancient city, it seemed right and proper.

Moscow is an historical city still faithful to the ancient, attractive, circular-radial pattern of its streets in spite of twentieth-century bungled redevelopment. Although some bombs were dropped in the autumn of 1941, the city was happily spared the disastrous air bombardment of the Second World War that so devastated some European cities. Nor has it been unduly subjected to destructive invaders. The German armies were halted on the outskirts of Moscow in 1941, although the Poles in the early seventeenth century and the French in 1812 left their mark. Napoleon's troops, only in residence for thirty-three days, witnessed the great Fire of Moscow when the city burned for six days and two-thirds of its houses were turned to ash. From the fourteenth century the most important churches had been built of stone and although blackened and damaged, they survived the Fire along with some of the brick and stone classical mansions erected only twenty years earlier. It was at this time that the predominantly wooden city began the metamorphosis into one of brick and stone.

The Moscow of the post-Fire period became one of the most attractive cities in Europe with fine neo-classical public buildings and small, comfortable houses decorated with pretty mouldings in the Russian Empire style. Their soft-hued interiors centred upon a suite of reception rooms with Ionic columns, restrained plaster work, painted ceilings and charming alcoves. Streets of these pleasant, ochre-coloured houses were set against the handsome, asymetrical seventeenth-century churches which stood on nearly every corner of the old part of the city. The rich world of orthodoxy reigned within these churches, the sumptuous gold of the iconostasis and the warmly painted walls and ceilings seen through a haze of incense. A surprising number of them still stand among the post-1812 small houses. Run-down and neglected for many decades, these churches are now slowly being restored and improved. With the recent renaissance in religion some are being reopened as places of worship, their church furniture replaced, frescoes newly painted, and bells put back in the long-empty belfries.

Interrupting the calm gentility of these neo-classical streets are the thrusting turrets and bizarre forms of the houses built for the nouveaux riches merchants at the end of the nineteenth century when any and every style was arbitrarily borrowed and combined to obtain the most extravagant effect. By that time merchants were replacing the gentry as the major patrons not only of architecture but also of the visual arts and even of music. Their sudden wealth following upon the liberation of the serfs (1861) and the opening up of new markets to the east with the construction of the railways, resulted in a new and vital force descending upon the city. Being only second- or third-generation serfs, they wanted something new and idiosyncratic to advertise their arrival in society; something totally different from the classicism associated with the nobility.

They found it first in eclecticism and then in the new architecture, Art Nouveau. Thus a novel element was introduced to Moscow's streets; curving lines, friezes, window frames at variance with one another. The interiors of these large houses and mansions were most sumptuously and creatively decorated by the finest craftsmen and with the best natural materials that Moscow could provide. The architect himself would design not only the flowing staircases, the unique fireplaces and parquet flooring, but also details such as the central heating vents, as seen in the Derozhinskaya Mansion where even the original upholstery was the work of the architect. Fortunately, Moscow did not lack talented builders and as a result the city is enriched with work by Fyodor Shekhtel, Lev Kekushev and William Walcot.

In the early years of the twentieth century, the new architectural fashion was quickly spent and a revival of neo-classicism became the vogue. It was interrupted by the First World War and then, in 1917, by the Revolution. Although fighting went on in Moscow for a week (whereas in St Petersburg it was all over in a day), buildings were not seriously harmed except for some damage to the old citadel, the Kremlin. It was here that the new Government set up office. For a brief, exciting spell a new architecture associated with the Revolution emerged, the unadorned, geometrical forms of the avant-garde or constructivism. Once again a fresh element was added to Moscow's skyline; cubes and cylinders, cantilevered floors and glass towers. These were incorporated into workers' clubs, factories and office buildings and a surprising number of them still stand. Among them is the idiosyncratic house of leading architect, Konstanin Melnikov, formed of two interlocking cylinders.

The experiments of the avant-garde, however, were too extreme for the successors to Lenin, and under Stalin they were harshly suppressed. Architecture thus returned to classicism, a style to which the Russians are constantly drawn, but its manifestation in the 1930s, 40s and 50s was the monumental, the grand and self-important. Significantly, ordinary housing was shamefully neglected. The stamp of the period is accurately felt in the inordinate grandeur of the metro stations, in the high-rise 'wedding-cake' towers of the late 40s and early 50s of which the New University is the most striking, and in many other sombre buildings with columns and pediments. But with time and the waning of this style of architecture after the death of Stalin, the buildings appear to have mellowed and today are acceptable as an integral part of the landscape. More modern buildings are less fussy but public buildings such as the Palace of Youth are distinctly in the Soviet grand style.

Thus Moscow offers a wealth of interiors which, until now, have remained almost entirely unknown and undiscovered. For Soviet as well as Western art historians, many of the treasures within these houses are a revelation. It is astonishing to find the interiors so relatively untouched in the seventy years since the Revolution and to discover classical or Gothic eighteenth-century rooms so faithfully and beautifully restored in recent times. Although it is undoubtedly true that Moscow has lost many magnificent buildings as a result of the iconoclastic reconstruction since the 1930s, and from sheer decay caused by time and lack of care, what remains is of intense architectural and historical interest. It is only now in the new conditions prevailing in the Soviet Union that they can be properly appreciated.

The radical changes wrought by the new spirit in the Soviet Union are themselves like a new revolution. *Perestroika* and *glasnost*, introduced in 1985, have taken a while to infiltrate the naturally suspicious officialdom of the Soviet Union, but by 1990 had become accepted at nearly all levels of society. It was precisely at this moment that we set out to explore and record the more interesting of the interiors of the great, individual buildings of Moscow's past and present. We arrived in the city full of trepidation and began simply by knocking on doors and asking for permission to photograph. Although we encountered many difficulties – unwired premises, the propensity of Russians to forget prearranged appointments, security of the camera equipment – these were all capable of solution. The blank wall of bureaucratic obstruction, which we fully expected to be our greatest problem, was rarely encountered and when it was was also overcome, albeit with a bit of ingenuity. We thus were able to realize our ambition of providing photographs of stunning but hitherto unknown buildings and to give a remarkably full and representative sample of the periods and styles of Moscow's architecture.

The book illustrates a variety of interiors: churches, most of them functioning, of different periods with their rich colour and carving; old cramped palaces as ornately decorated inside as the churches; grand rooms of noble mansions; amazingly creative baroque and gothic halls; the superb and individual styles of Art Nouveau; the economy of the constructivist style; the grandeur of the highly decorated metro stations; some fine examples of Soviet neo-classicism and of more recent buildings. We also photographed the interiors of ordinary Russian apartments with their inhabitants.

What was most surprising and gratifying was the exceptional kindness of most of the Russians encountered in our endeavour. In many cases we had only to ask and everything was put at our disposal. Russians are essentially sympathetic people and when personal contact is made barriers are removed. But above all it is the new climate prevailing in the USSR which made it possible for us to achieve what we have done. Perhaps this is best exemplified by the director of one of the shops photographed. Up some stairs, behind an intimidating gold plaque past the secretary was the director eating a sandwich at his empty desk. When the request was made, he smiled, took out his diary and quickly suggested a date. Astonished at the ease with which it had been arranged we were struck dumb. 'I can see you are surprised,' he said, 'but you must remember, this is *perestroika*.'

GLOSSARY

apse: the eastern recess in a church, usually semicircular, containing the altar.

barbican: the outer structure defending the entrance to a castle, fortress or kremlin.

basilica: an oblong Roman public building with colonnades and a semicircular apse, later sometimes converted to churches.

boyars: medieval Russian noblemen in the service of the grand princes and Tsars. The rank was abolished in the reign of Peter the Great.

bas-relief: shallow carving or sculpture on a background.

cartouche: ornamental panel usually in the form of a scroll with an illustration or inscription.

caryatid: a sculptured figure used as a column or pilaster.

coffered: regular sunken squares on a ceiling.

Constructivism: avant-garde art and architectural movement in the USSR in the 1920s based on function and geometrical forms.

cupola: onion- or helmet-shaped dome on the roof of an Orthodox church or chapel.

Deesis row: the third and central tier of an iconostasis with Christ in Majesty occupying the central position.

entablature: the part of the architectural order above the column or pilaster.

finials: formal ornament at the top of roof, gable, screen, etc.

fresco: wall-painting in water-colour on wet plaster.

frieze: horizontal broad band of sculpture or decoration either in entablature or elsewhere.

gabions: wicker basket filled with earth to provide wall fortifications.

Gaudiesque: like Gaudi, the Spanish architect (1852-1926) of freely planned churches and houses of Barcelona with extravagant excrescences.

glasnost: openness, the policy of greater frankness and honesty in public affairs as opposed to the secretiveness that characterized the Stalin and post-Stalin period.

Gosplan: the Soviet state planning organ that oversees all aspects of industrial production.

gostinny dvor: storehouses for merchants' wares in old Russia, latterly an arcade.

grisaille: painting executed in a series of greys.

grotto: artificial cavern, often decorated with rocks and shells, popular in the eighteenth century.

GUM: State Universal Store, the main department of Moscow on Red Square.

icon: (Greek – image) religious painting on wood panel venerated by orthodox believers in churches and homes.

iconostasis: tall screen divided into horizontal bands of icons that separate the altar from the main body of the church.

kokoshniki: semicircular or ogee-shaped decorative gables often placed in tiers.

Komsomol: Communist Youth League.

Lenin Plan of Monumental Propaganda: the decree of Lenin in 1918 to decorate Moscow and Leningrad with sculptures of revolutionary and socialist figures for the first anniversary of the Revolution.

Metropolitan: senior churchman ranking between an archbishop and the patriarch in the Russian Orthodox Church.

Moscow baroque: late seventeenth-century architectural style influenced by western baroque using white stone ornamental carving often on a red brick background.

neo-Russian: reworking of Russian traditional architecture in a new and interesting way at the end of the nineteenth century.

nomenklatura: the higher echelons of Government and Party whose appointments are controlled by the Communist Party.

ogee: double curve line bending first one way, then the other.

Patriarch: head of the Russian Orthodox Church.

pediment: finish to a classical façade over the portico or over windows and doors, usually triangular.

pendule: suspended ornament often encountered in Russian medieval architecture.

perestroika: literally 'restructuring' – refers to Gorbachev's reform policy introduced in 1985-6.

piloti: stilts to carry a building leaving the ground floor open – typical of Le Corbusier's architecture.

Potemkin Villages: the fake villages specially constructed in 1787 by Prince Potemkin along the Dnieper River to impress the Empress Catherine as she journeyed south to view New Russia. Thus it has come to mean putting on a false front.

rayon: Soviet municipal district.

refectory: in Russian church architecture refectory or 'trapeznaya' refers to the entrance hall or ante-room of the church.

Russian Empire: the later or mature classical style which prevailed in Russia from 1812 to the 1840s. It was more decorative than the severe Russian classicism of the late eighteenth century.

rusticated: stone blocks usually on the ground floor separated by deep joints giving a rich texture.

sarcophagus: an ornamental stone coffin.

sconce: a bracket for holding candles or lights on the wall.

socialist realism: the political theory of art imposed by Stalin and his successors. Its leitmotifs were optimism, patriotism, positive heroes and reality 'in its revolutionary development' i.e. subordinated to ideological purposes.

terem: the top floor or tower chamber of a medieval Russian house usually used as the women's quarters.

tessellated: a floor or wall decorated by small cubes of glass, stone or marble as in mosaic.

vault: an arched ceiling or roof of stone, brick, wood or plaster.

votive church: constructed to celebrate a military victory or important event.

6A. Terem Palace: the Throne Room is the principal room of the palace.

THE KREMLIN AND KITAI-GOROD

Moscow at first sight can seem a drab, dull city with large, pompous buildings lining wide, uninviting avenues which the pedestrian scurries across trying to avoid the fast, heavy traffic. It is therefore all the more astonishing to find at the centre a glittering fortress, high red-brick crenellated walls and imposing gates and, above the walls, a forest of golden crosses and cupolas of diverse size and height. The roughly triangular citadel is, of course, the Kremlin. Visible from afar, on the high bank of the Moskva River, the Kremlin is the true heart of Russia, the history both of the early Tsars

7A. St Basil's: the gallery, a detail.

and of the twentieth-century Communist state writ large upon its buildings. In medieval times the rulers of Muscovy, the Grand Dukes and Tsars and their henchmen, the powerful boyars, the leading churchmen, the metropolitans and patriarchs and, finally, the chancelleries of the Tsars, were all located within these walls. Again, in the 1920s and 30s, the Kremlin housed not only the new Party and government leaders and their offices, but their wives and children and hangers-on. With the rise of Stalin and the reign of terror, the very word 'Kremlin' took on a sinister connotation which, with the policy of *glasnost*, is only now receding.

From its origins as a simple stockade the Kremlin had by the fourteenth century become a fair citadel with churches and stone walls built by Grand Duke Dmitry Donskoi. The time of Ivan III in the late fifteenth century was the period of its greatest development although every age has left its imprint on the Kremlin. Ivan III with his Byzantine bride invited Italian masters and builders to come to Moscow to rebuild the old, decaying Kremlin. It was they, foreigners of the High Renaissance, who created this quintessentially Russian fortress. They built the magnificent brick walls, crenellated in the northern Italian fashion, with their twenty towers and barbican. They also built two of the greatest cathedrals and the Faceted Palace — the Tsars' audience chamber. Nevertheless, it was the Russian style they were instructed to recreate with the regulation five cupolas. Their contribution was their skill as engineers, their superior

technical knowledge, and it is significant that so much of what they built survives today.

The Kremlin is synonymous with the most important events of Russian history up to the time of Peter the Great. The long and dreadful reign in the sixteenth century of Ivan the Terrible led to the Time of Troubles and invasion of the Poles. This nadir in the fortunes of Russia was followed in the seventeenth century by the appearance of the new Romanov Dynasty. The relatively peaceful reigns of Mikhail and Aleksei saw an unprecedented flowering of art and architecture in which the Tsar's picturesque Terem Palace was built and the steeply pitched pyramid mounts added to the Kremlin towers. Only one of the boyars' palaces survives from this time, the Miloslavsky or Pleasaunce (later lived in by Stalin).

The reign of Aleksei was also the era of Nikon, the most powerful of the patriarchs, who ruled conjointly with the Tsar, and built for himself a sumptuous palace more magnificent than the Tsar's. Nikon overstretched himself and fell from favour; in his zeal to introduce liturgical reforms he caused the great schism in the Orthodox Church between the faithful and the Old Believers which has never been healed.

At the beginning of the eighteenth century, Peter the Great saw Russia's future in terms of the advances of western Europe and decided to abandon the old capital and build a new one on the swamps of the Neva River by the Baltic Sea. The 'Purple-clad Dowager', as Pushkin called Moscow, was left to decline and the Kremlin palaces fell into decay. Nevertheless, the huge trapezoidal Arsenal, typically a military building, was fitted into the north corner of the Kremlin in Peter's time. Although the Kremlin was no longer the seat of the Tsar or the political centre, all coronations continued to take place in the Assumption Cathedral and Moscow was commonly known as the second capital. During coronations a huge river of people flowed to Moscow along the rutted road from St Petersburg. Some of the emperors and empresses who followed Peter appeared to favour Moscow; the

Empress Anna stayed for two years (1730-31) before returning to her northern capital, but complained that accommodation in the Kremlin was most uncomfortable.

Moscow began to recover its position in the latter half of the eighteenth century, particularly after Peter III, Catherine's ill-fated husband, abolished obligatory state service. The nobility were thus able to leave St Petersburg and move to Moscow. Within the Kremlin, classical architecture made its first appearance with the coolly sedate Senate building, now the Council of Ministers, built in 1787 by Matvei Kazakov. In 1812 Napoleon invaded Moscow and made his residence in the Kremlin until the Great Fire forced him to flee. Before his hasty departure explosives were set in some of the Kremlin towers and the cathedrals were heavily looted – although Cossacks recovered many of the valuables when harassing the fleeing French.

Nicholas I, the most austere and reactionary of the Tsars, commissioned the eclectic Great Kremlin Palace in 1850 with over 700 rooms and grand halls eclipsing the old Terem palaces. It was rarely used, however, until the arrival of the Bolsheviks in 1918. In 1898 a heavy, Gothic statue of Alexander II was unveiled on the brow of the Kremlin Hill near the spot where the statue of Lenin now stands – it was demolished in 1918.

The Kremlin saw the twentieth century ushered in with a violence that foreshadowed later times. In 1905 the unpopular Governor-General, the Grand Duke Sergei, was assassinated by a bomb inside the Nikolsky Gate. During the Revolution itself Moscow witnessed a week of fighting that was centred around the Kremlin held by White troops who were eventually overpowered. In the process some of the churches and other buildings were damaged.

In March 1918, Moscow again became the capital of the new Soviet state and the new government, transferred from Petrograd, occupied the Kremlin as a matter of course. The buildings of the Kremlin in the 20s became not only the offices of the Executive Committee and Peoples' Commissariat, but also home to dozens of Bolsheviks and their families. The old buildings had not seen such comings and goings since the seventeenth century. By the mid-30s the population declined, atlhough Stalin kept a flat in the old Senate until his death. It was only after Stalin's death, that, in 1955, the Kremlin was again opened to the public.

The old citadel has suffered many changes since 1917. In the late 20s and 30s the Nicholas Palace, the Monastery of the Miracles, the Ascension Convent and the oldest church in Moscow, the Saviour in the Wood, were destroyed and the Great Kremlin Palace altered to accommodate Party Congresses and other meetings. In 1961 the only modern building of the Kremlin, the glass and concrete Palace of Congresses, was completed destroying in the process a number of eighteenth- and nineteenth-century offices and barracks. The new building was, however, sunk deeply into the ground to prevent it from overwhelming the familiar Kremlin skyline.

KITAI-GOROD

Kitai-Gorod adjoins the Kremlin to the north and east in a roughly rectangular shape ending at the Moskva River. The name may mean 'middle city' or it may refer to the woven baskets like gabions which, when filled with earth, reinforced the walls. It certainly does not mean Chinatown as some would have it (*Kitai* means China in modern Russian). The district was from the earliest times a lively market-place, a characteristic it retains to this day with the large and magnificent department store, GUM, situated on the periphery of Red Square. Wide walls were built in 1535-8 under the supervision of another Italian, Petrok Maly, to surround Kitai-Gorod only fifty years after the Kremlin walls were constructed. They enclosed a district then mainly populated by boyars and the clergy; craftsmen were settled outside its walls. To this day the remains of four monasteries can be seen, together with several ancient churches and houses including the vivid Trinity '*v Nikitnikakh*', and the fifteenth/sixteenth-century former Romanov House and the English Ambassadors' stone house.

Moscow was always the central market for Russia even after St Petersburg was founded and merchants travelled from afar to bring their goods to Kitai-Gorod. Red Square persisted for long as a market-place, although the Tsars periodically tried to expel the traders, preferring to keep it as a public square where decrees were announced or executions carried out. In 1555 the striking and bizarre form of St Basil's Cathedral was erected by order of Ivan the Terrible, not in the Kremlin, but in Red Square to celebrate his victory over the Tatars at Kazan. In the eighteenth century the first masonry arcade was built on the edge of the square and in 1893 the present GUM building was constructed on the same spot. In 1883 the History Museum was added to the northern end of Red Square, a romantic reflection of the unique design of St Basil's which it faces. In 1929 the black and dark red permanent mausoleum which contains Lenin's body was built in front of the Senate Tower. Fulfilling the function of a tribune too, it fits tactfully enough into the scheme of the square which thus acquired its present form.

In the nineteenth century Kitai-Gorod became the business and financial centre of Russia as an unprecedented expansion of manufacture and markets occurred. In the early nineteenth century a huge building, the Gostiny Dvor, an arcaded block with Corinthian capitals on the pilasters, provided accommodation for visiting merchants and their wares. A stock market opened in a fine building on Ilinka (Kuibyshev) Street which in today's changing world may be reactivated. At the turn of the century, banks and other financial institutions proliferated in Kitai-Gorod and it began to take on something of the appearance of the City of London.

The southern sector was less developed and, before the Revolution, was something of a slum area although many fine churches and ancient buildings could be found there. After the Revolution the whole district was demolished to build the projected Palace of Industry. Happily, the old street of churches and medieval buildings opposite St Basil's was not pulled down. At this time nearly all the medieval walls of the district, which had survived almost intact, were also demolished and the brick was used to help build the new metro. However, the project for the Palace of Industry was abandoned. In the 1960s a gigantic hotel, the Rossiya, was erected on the site occupying the entire area by the river. Originally planned to be thirty-six storeys high, it was fortunately reduced, after Khrushchev's removal, to the less offensive twelve.

1A. Assumption Cathedral: the Last Judgement occupies the west wall and, above, the Transfiguration.

· 1 ·

THE ASSUMPTION CATHEDRAL

The Assumption Cathedral forms part of the incomparable ensemble in the central square of three great cathedrals, the tall bell-tower of Ivan Veliky, and the Great Kremlin Palace with the ancient palaces and churches within its walls. It is the most beautiful place in Moscow.

The Kremlin, although the embodiment of everything Russian, was largely built by Italians in the late fifteenth century, and the Assumption Cathedral, erected in 1475-9, was no exception. The Bolognese architect/engineer Ridolfo (Aristotle) Fioravanti was most tactful in combining Russo/Byzantine design with superior Italian engineering, and his church is more spacious and grander than Russian domestic churches of the period. His Italian eye must have been offended by the voluptuous apses of the Russian churches for he did not allow such asymmetry in the Assumption Cathedral where the apse extrusion is discreetly included within the rectangular form of the building. Fioravanti's reward for his success in constructing the first church of Muscovy was to be thrown into prison by the Tsar in 1485 when he begged permission to return to Italy. He died there a year later.

The Assumption Cathedral is historically the premier church in Russia although it ceased to be a functioning church in 1918. All coronations of the Tsars took place within its walls even after the move to St Petersburg. The cathedral traditionally has served as a museum of the best and most honoured of Russia's icons. The revered twelfth-century icon of the Virgin of Vladimir was located in the lower left of the iconostasis; replaced with a fifteenth-century copy the icon now hangs in the Tretyakov Gallery. The icons line the walls in chronological order and together provide a clear and easily understood history of the development of the art in Russia.

The cathedral was first the church of the metropolitans, and then, after the patriarchate was established in 1589, became the church of the patriarchs. It serves as their

1B. Assumption Cathedral: a view of the Ascension depicted on the interior of the central cupola.

burial place and the walls are lined with magnificent sarcophagi of most of the metropolitans and patriarchs. A special wrought-iron enclosure made in 1625 contains holy relics and the body of Metropolitan Hermogenes who starved to death rather than submit during the Polish occupation in 1610.

It is a matter of historical irony that in 1917 the newly elected Patriarch, Tikhon, barely had time to establish himself in his splendid, ancient seat when the sound of gun fire was heard from the Red Guards moving in on the Kremlin. For over seventy years thereafter no services were held in the cathedral. But *perestroika* has reached the Kremlin itself; in November 1989, the Soviet authorities allowed a service to be held in the Assumption Cathedral in honour of the tercentenary of the founding of the Russian patriarchate. It seems possible that the cathedral will once again witness great religious occasions, if not formal state ceremonials.

· 2 ·

THE ARCHANGEL CATHEDRAL

The Cathedral of the Archangel Michael on the south-eastern side of Cathedral Square, facing the Annunciation Cathedral, was built as the burial place of the rulers of Muscovy. Its tombs contain nearly all the rulers up to the time of Peter the Great when St Petersburg was founded (1703). It was the last of the great churches of the Kremlin to be built by Italian architects (Alevisio Novi, 1505-8) and, unlike the others, its façade is clearly decorated in the style of the Renaissance.

The cathedral, on the edge of the ravine facing the Moskva River, also differs in design from the other Kremlin churches with which it is contemporary. Not the usual cube, it is elongated on its east-west axis and the five cupolas, four surrounding the central gold dome, are sited closer to the eastern end, giving it a rather disturbing lack of balance. It also displays novel Italianate features such as the distinctive Venetian scallop shells in the upper gables. Equally novel is the grand western portal

2. Archangel Cathedral: the white figure of Christ inside the cupola surveys the iconostasis.

richly carved with intricate floral ornamentation.

In contrast to the façade, the interior architecture is rather outdated with six heavy columns (two behind the iconostasis) taking up a large part of the narrow space. The narrowness of the nave, where little light filters through the slit windows, is further enhanced by the many tombs of grand princes and Tsars grouped around the columns and in the aisles. The tombs are of stone carved in the seventeenth century and covered in 1903 with handsome bronze covers on which the names of the deceased and their dates stand out in relief.

The Archangel Michael, whose exploits are depicted in the frescoes, was considered a help and comfort in military battles and it is appropriate that the burial church of the Tsars should be dedicated to him. The colour combinations are quite unusual, soft greens, reds and light metallic blue; happily the paint has not markedly deteriorated.

· 3 ·

THE ANNUNCIATION CATHEDRAL

The golden-headed Annunciation Cathedral, the Royal Chapel of the Tsar and his family, is smaller than the other cathedrals in the square. Unlike them, it was not built by Italians, but Russians, and is more intimate and mysterious, more quintessentially Russian than the grander cathedrals.

In 1484 master-builders from Pskov were invited to Moscow by Ivan III to rebuild the old, decaying family chapel linked to the palaces of the medieval Kremlin. A century after it was first built with three cupolas, the originally open gallery was enclosed allowing for six more. The resulting nine and the roofs were then sheeted in gold to become the dominant feature of the richly attired church as we know it today.

The cathedral is also closely associated with Ivan the Terrible. The Church was often at odds with this intemperate Tsar but even Ivan, who in some ways revered the Church, dare not oppose it entirely and in 1572, when he married for the fourth time, he was barred from attending services within the building (the Orthodox Church sanctions only three marriages) and had to remain in a specially constructed south porch behind a grille.

The mysterious interior of the Annunciation with its superb paintings and icons is as majestic as the exterior. The gallery-porch takes up a large part of the available space and within the church proper there is almost a feeling of claustrophobia, relieved only by the height of the building which leads upward into the underside of the domes. It is dense with paintings on every inch of wall and column, and high up is the sight of Christ Pantocrator looking down from the central dome.

The most remarkable feature of the cathedral, however, is the wall of religious paintings, the iconostasis, which screens the altar from the nave. The iconostasis, which originated in the fourteenth century from the low Byzantine altar rail, relayed in pictorial form the liturgy of the Church to what was then a largely illiterate populace. It received its highest development in Russia in this unsurpassed example.

Traditionally, within an iconostasis, the icons are grouped in tiers. The lowest contains those of local significance which include the depiction of the festival after which the church is dedicated (in this case the Annunciation). Above this a row of icons illustrates the months. The majestic third, Deesis row, then appears (bottom row in picture) which provides the main focus of the iconostasis with Christ in the centre flanked by the Virgin on his right and John the Baptist on his left. Next to John the Baptist and the Virgin are the Archangels Gabriel and Michael respectively, and beyond them disciples and other saints all inclining to the central figure. Above the Deesis row is the splendid Festival row of fifteen icons illustrating the main events of the Church year. The top row depicts the prophets, with small pictures of the patriarchs in the ogee-shaped finials to the iconostasis.

Three of the greatest icon painters of all time contributed to this work of art. Theophanes the Greek, the superb artist who came from Constantinople to Novogorod, was responsible for its overall design and himself painted the marvellous elongated figures in the Deesis row. He was assisted by Prokhor of Gorodets and by the young Andrei Rublyev who is credited with many of the wonderful icons in the Festival row. Rublyev became the most

supremely inspired religious artist of Russia, his gentle monumental figures executed with a delicacy of line and harmony of colour unseen before or after his time. The icon frame was executed in gilt bronze work by N.V. Sultanov in 1890; the original frame would have been wooden.

This convention, with many variations, was established in the fourteenth century, reach its apogee in the sixteenth and first half of the seventeenth centuries; in the eighteenth and following centuries the style became far more decorative. It is nothing short of a miracle that this iconostasis has survived through the centuries. According to the chronicles it was painted in 1405 and transferred to the new cathedral in 1489. After the Fire of 1547 the original paintings were presumed to have perished but they were merely painted over in oils and in 1918-29 under Igor Grabar, the great art historian and restorer, the early icons were discovered, cleaned and restored.

· 4 ·

THE FACETED PALACE

On one side of Cathedral Square at the heart of the Kremlin, the ancient Faceted Palace presents its east wall of rusticated stone facings in the form of diamond facets. It now seems unobtrusive but when first built by the Italians, Marco Ruffo and Pietro Solario in 1487-91, it was a more prominent edifice within the ensemble of cathedrals, bell-tower and palaces. Over time it has lost both its steeply pitched gilded roof which once enhanced its stature and its supremacy on the surrounding skyline.

The palace was built as an audience hall for the Tsars. With the Holy Vestibule, which provides its entrance, it is the only surviving part of the ancient palace built by Ivan III. Above the basement level it consists of one large, almost square, chamber supported by a central, massive pillar that fans out into four vaults. The chamber is 27 metres square and 9 metres high at its highest point. At the base of the pillar

3. Annunciation Cathedral: the splendid Deesis row is dominated by Christ in Majesty.

shelves were once positioned which served to display the gold and silver plate of the royal household on grand occasions. Here Ivan the Terrible received ambassadors from his throne on the north-east side, with his boyars in tall hats ranged along the walls on benches. He presumably received here the English merchant adventurer, Richard Chancellor, who made his way to Moscow in 1553 having arrived at Kholmogory on the White Sea while on his way to China. The China venture forgotten, he quickly made a deal with the Tsar and the Muscovy Company was born under which England was to have a monopoly of trade with Russia for a century – only abrogated when Charles I was beheaded. In the hall, too, on Christmas Day in 1557, Antony Jenkinson, the intrepid traveller and later English Ambassador, was one of the six hundred guests at a magnificent feast given by the dread Tsar.

Wall paintings of 1668 by the last of the master icon painters, Simon Ushakov, lost in the eighteenth century, were replaced in 1881 by two artists from the icon-painting village of Palekh. Ushakov's drawings were used to reproduce the overall design although the present large-figured paintings would appear to be a free interpretation of his work. In the 1960s the carving and gilt ornament of the entranceway from the Holy Vestibule and base of the pillar were replaced using the few fragments that had survived.

It is not hard to imagine state occasions in this airy chamber, or formal dinners with the Tsar alone at a raised table sitting on a high-backed throne. Below him, gentlemen of the court sat in order of rank and favour while servants busied themselves carrying dish after gold dish of various meats of which roast swan was the highlight. Dinner would begin with the Tsar himself in the Russian tradition proffering bread and salt to the most important guests watched by the Tsaritsa from an upper-level secret chamber. Today the Faceted Palace is still used to host formal receptions and to stage dinners for visiting dignitaries. In this hall Mrs Thatcher and President Reagan were entertained by Mr Gorbachev during their visits to Moscow. Roast swan is no longer served, nor does the Soviet head of state sit alone at table, but in other respects the tradition survives.

4. Faceted Palace: the great pillar upholds the painted vaulted ceiling.

5. Great Kremlin Palace: A: doorways off the Holy Vestibule lead to the Bolshoi, Terem and Faceted Palaces. C: the octagonal room of St Vladimir's Hall.

· 5 ·

THE GREAT KREMLIN PALACE

Nicholas I, an austere, conservative ruler obsessed with military order, harboured a sneaking admiration for the ancient, slavic traditions of Moscow so different from the sophisticated, western attitudes of St Petersburg. In 1837 he commissioned a new royal palace in the Kremlin in national Russian style from the architect, Konstantin Ton. The Tsar, with his motto of autocracy, orthodoxy, and Russian nationalism, found his ideal architect in Ton who, although a St Petersburg architect trained in the classical style, evolved a Russo-Byzantine historical manner.

The old residence of the Tsars was a mixture of various chambers, chapels and

service buildings, a picturesque ensemble haphazardly joined together by passageways and bridges. In contrast to the ordered cool grace of column and pediment in northern St Petersburg, the old palaces seemed small and run-down and entirely unsuitable for use as imperial residences. In planning the new palace for Nicholas, Ton nevertheless decided to incorporate several of the remaining old palaces (although he also demolished some important medieval buildings). These were renovated, repainted and brought back to life again after a long period of neglect. Thus the survival of the oldest part of the Kremlin is in part due to the construction of the new palace. Access to the old palaces can only be obtained by traversing the long halls of the Great Kremlin Palace.

Intended as the Imperial residence in Moscow, the ground floor contains the

5B. Great Kremlin Palace: St George's Hall is used for the most important occasions.

private rooms of the Tsar and his family. An impressive State Staircase of artificial marble leads to the principal floor and the five main halls each dedicated to one of the Orders of the Empire. The white Hall of St George was originally the largest hall; the order was established in 1769 and was the highest military decoration in the Russia of the Tsars. The hall is used for receptions and the presentation of orders and medals; in 1961 the first cosmonaut, Yuri Gagarin, was received in this hall after his historic trip into space. It is here that the President greets visiting Heads of State.

In the smaller adjoining Hall of St Vladimir (an Order of 1782), built over the old Boyars' Court, international treaties are usually signed.

6B. Terem Palace: the Cross Chamber where the Tsar would receive ambassadors.

6C. Terem Palace: the bedchamber of the Tsars with florid nineteenth-century decoration.

· 6 ·

· 6 ·

THE TEREM PALACE

The oldest buildings in the Kremlin are those that comprise the Terem Palace, the Tsars' residence until Peter the Great moved the capital to St Petersburg in 1703. *Terem* means tower-chamber and the principal rooms of the palace, a complex edifice that evolved haphazardly, are set high in the upper levels of the tiered structure and include a number of equally randomly placed small churches and chapels. In 1837, under the supervision of F.G. Solntsev, they were decorated in a fanciful recreation of the seventeenth century; even the splendid tiled stoves are reproductions. Regrettably the churches and palaces cannot be seen from Cathedral Square nor viewed by the public, although glimpses of the upper tiers can be obtained from the Moskva River or the Great Stone Bridge.

The palaces came into being as new living quarters were required by each succeeding Tsar or his wife. The various chambers, usually wooden, were built on the high stone basements erected by the Italian architects at the end of the fifteenth century. The Tsars preferred the comfort and warmth of wooden palaces, but fire was such a hazard that the first Romanov, Mikhail, resolved to rebuild his palace of stone. The Terem Palace was thus erected in 1635-6 in succeeding tiers by Antip Konstantinov and Larion Ushakov. The older sections, including the workshops of the Kremlin craftsmen and the Tsarina's Golden Chamber, were incorporated into the new building which rested on the fifteenth-century basement.

To enter the personal apartments of the Tsars, on the fourth and fifth storeys, one must follow a circuitous route. The rooms consist of the Boyars' waiting-room, or ante-room, followed by the Cross or Reception Chamber, where the Tsar would hold audiences with the boyars. The third room, the Throne Room, has the most elaborate exterior window ornamentation which is known as the Petition Window. From here a box would be lowered and petitions placed in it; it was called the 'Longtime Box' because of delays in

6D. Terem Palace: the ante-room where boyars waited on the Tsar's pleasure.

responding to the petitions. This is followed by the bedchamber. The narrow *Freilina* or Ladies in Waiting Corridor passes along all the rooms; this was traditionally the place where selected virgins from noble families would be paraded for the scrutiny of the Tsar who would choose one as his bride; Ivan the Terrible utilized this method at least seven times.

It is something of a miracle that these churches and palaces have survived at all considering the major rebuilding that has occurred in every century, and the contempt of both Stalin and Khrushchev for Russia's architectural heritage.

7. St Basil's. B: interior of the cupola of the central church of the Intercession of the Virgin. C: a view of the Virgin and Child in a cupola.

· 7 ·

ST BASIL'S CATHEDRAL

There is possibly no other building in Moscow that so encapsulates the Russian national character as the Cathedral of the Intercession on the Moat (popularly known as St Basil's, named after the holy fool who was admired by Ivan the Terrible and is buried in its wall), that curious medley of shapes and colours that to the western eye seem innately oriental, mysterious and idiosyncratic. Yet, the architecture of this important votive church has its own rationale and place in the development of Russian architecture.

The young Ivan IV, not yet the Terrible, had early in his reign taken the ancient city of Kazan, a stronghold of the once formidable Tatars, some 900 kilometres to the east of Moscow. The great victory occurred on the feast of Pokrov, the Intercession of the Virgin, one of the most highly regarded religious festivals of the Orthodox Church. To celebrate, Ivan determined to erect a great memorial church, not in the Kremlin where he retained childhood memories of rampaging boyars, but in the market-place of the city, Red Square, at the high point where it begins the descent towards the river. Completed in 1561, the architect designed it in the form of one central church surrounded by eight lesser chapels symbolizing the eight attempts to take Kazan.

The extraordinary variety of shapes, colours, textures and motifs derives from indigenous wooden architecture as it was expressed in the 1532 stone Church of the Ascension at the Tsars' palace at Kolomenskoe. Together with the neighbouring church of St John the Baptist, it served as the precursor of St Basil's with the octagon as the central form and the sharp arrow gable as the main motif.

7D. St Basil's: entering the narrow confines of the Cathedral.

The interior is a labyrinth in which the nine different churches are linked by very narrow corridors, with bright floral designs painted on the brick walls. Each chapel has a high tower open to the cupola constantly emphasizing the narrow confines of the churches, some with exceptionally fine iconostases.

St Basil's was the scene of the annual, colourful Palm Sunday procession which would emerge from the Saviour Gate of the Kremlin, the servers and acolytes carrying icons and singing. The Tsar, gorgeously robed, led the Patriarch's horse whose ears were lengthened to simulate an ass, portraying the entry of Christ into Jerusalem. They would process to St Basil's, sometimes also known as the Jerusalem Church, and enter for the service.

The cathedral was looted by Napoleon's troops in 1812, but restored soon afterwards. After the Revolution, it was closed for services and in 1929 became a branch of the State History Museum open to the public. However, it proved an irritation to Stalin. As St Basil's stands at the exit from Red Square, the annual military parades on the occasion of the anniversary of the Revolution have to divide to avoid the cathedral. Rumours began to circulate in Moscow in the early 1930s that the authorities were contemplating demolishing the cathedral as they had already so many others. Pyotr Baranovsky, the architect, who had recently restored the Kazan Cathedral by the History Museum at the opposite side of Red Square only to see it torn down, was so horrified at the idea of St Basil's meeting the same fate that he chained himself to the railings of the cathedral threatening to kill himself if the plan went ahead. He was removed from the railings and duly incarcerated in the Lubyanka, but, incredibly, his exceptionally brave act in those lawless times succeeded. The great cathedral was not torn down and he was released after eighteen months.

In October 1990, the celebration of the Feast of the Intercession of the Virgin was once again held in the cathedral for the first time since the Revolution. It was a moving sight to see candle-holding believers massed in Red Square, which for so long had been closed to religious manifestations.

....

7E. St Basil's: plain brick walls focus on the spiral design of the cupola.

8A. Romanov House: the boyar's study with wall coverings of gilded leather.

· 8 ·

THE HOUSE OF THE ROMANOV
BOYARS

From Varvarka (Razin) Street the House of the Romanov Boyars with its steeply pitched roofs, tower and wooden upper floor looks shabby, the dirt left by the grit of winter permanently clinging to it. This is both one of the oldest houses in Moscow and one of the best examples of creative rebuilding. The sixteenth-century steep stone basement built on an incline is genuine, as is the two-storey central section of the house built of brick in the seventeenth century, but the third section, the unusual wooden upper floor, was added in the mid-nineteenth century during fanciful 'restoration'.

The old hall belonged to the Romanov boyars, one of the most important sixteenth-century Moscow families. The young Tsar, Ivan Vasilievich (later the Terrible), chose as his first wife, Anastasia, a member of the Romanov clan. With her he seemed reasonably content, the more terrible part of his reign occurring after her sudden death, possibly by poisoning, in 1560. These royal connections helped when it came to the election of a new Tsar after the Poles had been expelled from the Kremlin in 1612. The boyars' choice fell on the sixteen-year-old Mikhail Romanov who allegedly wept when he heard the news and had to be persuaded to accept the honour.

8B. Romanov House: the elaborate stove for the upper wooden floor.

C

8. Romanov House: C: a faithful reconstruction of one of the sixteenth-century tiled stoves.
D: the wooden upper floor with loom, traditionally the women's quarters.

In the 1850s Alexander II became interested in the old house of his ancestors and requested that it be studied and restored as the House of the Romanov Boyars. The architect, F.F. Richter, decided to add a third, wooden section to the top of the house in the manner of the early medieval houses of the sixteenth century.

The whole, charming, rebuilt hall was opened in 1859 to the pubic and it is still a museum depicting boyar life in general. The interior, for all its artfulness, is completely credible. The deep basement is used to exhibit fascinating items from everyday life that have survived like bark shoes and bowls, wooden kitchen implements, horse fittings and weapons. Up the narrow stairs to the two-storied seventeenth-century section the rooms have been decorated to resemble a wealthy man's house of that time. The study is the most striking with its embossed leather wall coverings and magnificent tiled stove (it is a shock to discover the stove was only made in 1965). The ladies' rooms are equally fascinating; as they rarely ventured out of doors their life revolved around domestic activities especially sewing and embroidery.

D

9. *Trinity Church: A: south chapel fresco of the crucifixion of Peter. B: frescoes.*

· 9 ·

THE CHURCH OF THE TRINITY 'V NIKITNIKAKH'

The Church of the Trinity 'v Nikitnikakh' is in a small lane away from the main streets of Kitai-Gorod and to come upon its sumptuous soft red walls densely covered with white detail topped by a multitude of gables − the ogee-shaped *kokoshniki* − and, surmounting the whole, five full-blown shining green cupolas, is nothing less than astonishing. The sculpture of the portals, porch and gallery are similar to the Terem Palace and suggest that master craftsmen from the Kremlin workshops may have taken part in the construction. It is situated behind a building designed by the Art Nouveau architect, Fyodor Shekhtel, and in front of a modern block, both of which belong to the Central Committee of the Communist Party. These buildings, once held in great awe, seem most incongruous set against the riot of colour and shapes that is the vigorous architecture of the church.

The church was built in 1634 by a wealthy merchant from Yaroslavl, Grigory Nikitnikov, as his private church in the grounds of his Moscow residence. Nikitnikov was a member of the highest merchant guild, the *gosti*, of which there were not more than thirty members in all. This most privileged group acted as financial advisers to the Tsar and, in some cases, even collected customs duties for the regime, but were exempt from paying any themselves. They had unlimited right of travel, a highly prized privilege. However, they were still only merchants, not boyars, and had no right to live in the Kremlin. The closest Nikitnikov could get to the Court was to build his home in Kitai-Gorod.

The interior is as richly adorned as the façade. One of the artists of the splendid frescoes was Simon Ushakov, the last great icon painter before the introduction of perspective, whose studio was near by. The frescoes were painted in 1652-3 and reflect the influence of worldly art by the inclusion of portraits of the Nikitnikov family.

After the Revolution the church became a museum of architecture and painting of the seventeenth century under the umbrella of the History Museum.

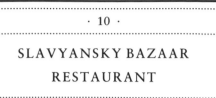

· 10 ·

SLAVYANSKY BAZAAR RESTAURANT

One of the more colourful restaurants in Moscow is the Slavyansky Bazaar on Nikolskaya (25th October) Street in Kitai-Gorod. Its richly painted, romantic, Russian interior blends well with the Russian cuisine – blini, caviar, chicken Kiev, mushrooms in sour cream – and the lively stage shows where portly *artistes* sing folksongs with great gusto accompanied by a band of musicians playing Russian folk instruments.

The restaurant came into being as the dining-room of the hotel Slavyansky Bazaar which was awarded first-class status in the 1914 edition of *Baedeker*. The hotel opened in 1872 and a year later the restaurant was built in the courtyard of the building by the reputable architect, A.E. Veber.

The restaurant and hotel were very popular among the *intelligentsia* of Moscow in those days. Among the more notable guests were Tchaikovsky and Chekhov. But the restaurant is best known for the famous meeting there on 21-22 June 1897 of Konstantin Stanislavsky and Vladimir Nemirovich-Danchenko, when the concept of the Moscow Arts Theatre was born. The two sat at one table for eighteen hours, from 2 p.m. to 8 a.m. the next morning, endlessly discussing the project. What is even more remarkable is that the restaurant tolerated their lengthy stay and did not throw them out. Stanislavsky in his memoirs comments: 'International conferences do not consider the world questions before them so closely as we considered the foundation of our future enterprise, the questions of pure art, our artistic ideals, scenic ethics, technique, the plans of organization, our future repertoire, and our mutual relations.'

Chekhov used the hotel as a setting for some of his short stories. In 'Lady with a Dog' the Slavyansky Bazaar Hotel is the venue for Anna Sergeyevna's desperate *rendez-vous* with her lover, Gurov, who first walks his daughter to school and then drops in at the hotel for their unhappy and hopeless tryst.

After the Revolution the hotel was closed and used to house various Soviet

10. Slavyansky Bazaar: the gaudy interior of the popular restaurant.

organizations. During the 'October Days' of the Revolution, Red Guards captured Nikolskaya (25th October) Street in their attack on the Kremlin and turned the restaurant into a soldiers' café. Later, the Soviet Civil Defence Society was located here. Vladimir Mayakovsky, in his poem 'No. 17', expresses the shock he felt at the sight of posters portraying the horrors of chemical warfare.

The famous restaurant came to life again in 1966 when it was renovated and repainted in the garish, neo-Russian style that had been popular at the turn of the century. Unlike many other restaurants in Moscow which seem to serve an almost exclusively foreign clientèle, the Slavyansky Bazaar is popular with Russians.

· 11 ·

GUM STATE UNIVERSAL STORE

From the earliest times the Tsars tried in vain to rid Red Square, the lively marketplace of Moscow, of its messy stalls, noisy traders and attendant crowds. Eventually the trading stalls were moved further away from the Kremlin wall, making the square better suited for the ceremonial and political occasions for which it is still best known today. The stalls nearest to the Kremlin, the Upper Trading Rows, sold the most important goods and it is they

11. GUM: *Moscow's most famous department store is lit from above by extensive ceiling lights.*

that have been transformed into the State Universal Store, GUM, Moscow's most famous shop.

Designed by Alexander Pomerantsev, and one of the first buildings to use reinforced concrete, it was opened in 1893 with three long, parallel passages off which a multitude of small shops or stalls, some 1,000 of them, were situated. The lighting for this enclosed market-place was most ingeniously provided. To the plans of the engineer, Vladimir Shukhov, unique roofs made up of iron struts and a 15-metre glass span, well ahead of their time, were constructed over each passage. The three halls, each painted a different colour — peppermint green, light blue, peach — are thus naturally lit and the effect is airy and spacious even when the crowds congregate. At the centre is a splendid wrought-iron fountain, and delightful wrought-iron bridges connect the upper stories across the passageways. Even the original brass central-heating vents are still in place.

If the interior of the great market-place is remarkable, the exterior with its long grey-stone façade ineptly parades the various motifs of old Russian architecture and the Byzantine inheritance. Unlike the History Museum across the way, built at the same time, it completely fails in its aim of providing an interesting foil to the Kremlin façade which it faces.

After the Revolution, renamed GUM, it continued to function as a shop until the late 1920s when it was turned into an office building for the burgeoning Soviet and Party bureaucrats of the first Five Year Plan and the collectivization of agriculture. The grand halls were also used for at least one lying-in-state. In 1932 Stalin's wife, Nadezhda Alliluyeva, in despair at her husband's policies, shot herself in their Kremlin flat. Stalin had her body laid out in the hall of what is now GUM and stayed by it day after day, his heavily lidded yellow eyes watching to see who came to pay their respects. One of the Soviet leaders, Ivan Moskvin, who had been in the highest echelons of the *nomenklatura*, refused to view the body though urged by his friends that it would be dangerous not to go; in 1937 he was arrested and shot, but then so too were most of the people who had faithfully filed past Alliluyeva's corpse in the central hall of GUM.

GUM was repaired and reopened in 1952 as the great emporium it was intended to be, and has flourished ever since.

· 12 ·

METRO PLOSHCHAD REVOLYUTSY (REVOLUTION SQUARE)

The first part of the Arbatsko-Pokrovskaya Line, the third of the metro lines to be built, was opened in 1938. The most renowned Soviet architects were engaged to construct the stations on the line. These contained remarkable, spacious halls, the 'palaces of the people', finished in rare marbles and decorated with statuary and mosaic panels. The station Ploshchad Revolyutsy is no exception. Its splendid hall was designed by Aleksei Dushkin who was also responsible for the exceptional Mayakovskaya station on the first line opened in 1935.

The impressive central hall with its great vaulted ceiling is punctuated with marble-lined arches leading onto the train platforms. They are decorated with thirty-six vigilant seated or crouching heroic figures in bronze by Matvei Manizer, personifying the defence and protection of Soviet power and the peaceful labour of Soviet people. This preoccupation with defence occurs again and again as the main theme in the metro stations, and it is surprising to learn that the stations were built sometime before the Second World War. However, it seems to be not only apprehension at Hitler's rise to power, but also part of the general political psychology of the time. Exaggeration of the threat to the Soviet state, a very real feeling in the early years of its existence, had by the 1930s become a convenient device to justify the show trials and reign of terror, in full spate when these stations were being built.

Matvei Manizer's style can be fairly described as academic. He was a popular sculptor in the Stalin and post-Stalin period when a great deal of statuary was being erected all over Moscow. It is interesting that of all the busts created in 1918 for Lenin's Plan of Monumental Propaganda only Manizer's relief 'The Worker' at the Petrovsky Arcade survives.

12. Metro Ploshchad Revolyutsy: Manizer's bronze figures guard the entrance to the platform.

13A. Chertkov Mansion: the west-wing staircase leading to the library.

EAST MOSCOW

13B. Chertkov Mansion: the White Hall.

East Moscow, between the busy shops and offices of Myasnitskaya (Kirov) Street and the Moskva River, is a quiet, residential area dotted with old disused churches, a few squat medieval houses, and street after street of quietly decaying ochre-coloured houses of the past two centuries. Some relief to the normally flat Moscow is obtained near the bank of the river where Ivanova Gorka (St John's Hill) is situated, one of the loveliest parts of the city. The old Convent of St John high on the steep hill on which little houses cling has excellent views, including one of a Stalin Gothic wedding-cake palace towering in the background.

Myasnitskaya is one of Moscow's principal avenues linking the three railway stations – the Leningrad, Yaroslavl and Kazan – to the centre. Its architecture ranges from the noble dignity of the classical Baryshnikov Mansion built at the end of the eighteenth century, through Empire and Art Nouveau to eclectic vagaries like the garish pseudo-Chinese Perlov tea shop. Le Corbusier's only building in Moscow – an unusual office block – with its uncompromisingly modern treatment adds to the variety of the street. The continuation of Myasnitskaya across the Garden Ring leads to the astonishing square of the three railway stations; one classical, one daringly *à la Russe* and one in conscious mimicry of the Kazan Kremlin. Underneath the railways rumble the vibrant, ornate stations of the metro.

Tucked in just behind Myasnitskaya near the Boulevard are two functioning churches, the Archangel Gabriel or Menshikov Tower and St Fyodor Stratilatus. The beautiful baroque sculptural form of the Menshikov Tower, built in 1707, is described by Alexander Pasternak, brother of the famous writer: ' . . . how changeable though uniformly beautiful its individual spire appears, lapped in the milky-pink, mother-of-pearl mists of winter dawns or the rich damson of the setting sun.' It was once the tallest building in Moscow; it can still be tantalizingly glimpsed from unexpected corners.

The Boulevard, which lovingly encircles the old city giving it a breathing corridor of green, plays a vital part in the landscape. Between it and the noisy, dirty highway which was shorn of its trees in 1937 and is the now grotesquely misnamed Garden Ring, is another quiet maze of narrow streets of old yellowing houses, apartment blocks of the last century, the occasional church, and great mansions. Of the latter, the splendours of the mansion of Aleksei Vikulevich Morozov stand out. This house, so ordinary from the outside, has great surprises in store for the unsuspecting visitor. Two architects of very different stamp, the famous Shekhtel of Art Nouveau fame and the more prosaic Chichagov, have both left their mark.

An old medieval mansion, the Yusupovs' Moscow home for two hundred years, was confiscated in 1918 by the new Soviet government. Its picturesque red and white façade adds colour to Bolshoi Kharitonevsky Lane and within it is a maze of small rooms and staircases all heavily painted and decorated in the fashion of the seventeenth century.

Where the snaking Yauza River empties into the Moskva the Gothic high-rise block of one of the Stalinist palaces sits astride the confluence of the waters. On the banks of the rivers is another of Moscow's most charming districts, the Zayauze, with six churches (two functioning), eighteenth-century mansions and the famous red brick Taganka Theatre, perhaps the best of the modern buildings in Moscow. Taganka Square, with its fine metro station of blue ceramics, is a square only in name; it is really just a heavily used dusty crossroads with no attempt at harmonious buildings or access for pedestrians. There is a horrendous plan to demolish the remaining nineteenth-century and earlier buildings on the periphery of the square and build faceless tower blocks, but the new city administration may prevent this from happening.

Further out across the Yauza River beyond the Garden Ring, a soldiers' colony set up by Peter the Great has bequeathed some fine buildings – the great classical Catherine Palace, now the Malinovsky Tank Academy, and some eighteenth- and nineteenth-century mansions and hospitals. On the west side of the Yauza a Foreigners' Settlement was founded in the middle of the seventeenth century to protect Muscovites from contamination by their heretical prayer houses. By an accident of fate, Peter the Great spent his childhood in the rambling royal palace at Preobrazhenskoe just across the Yauza opposite the settlement. He was immensely attracted to the orderliness and worldliness of the foreigners which subsequently influenced his future policy of opening Russia to the west.

With the rapid expansion of industry in Moscow in the nineteenth century, the site of Peter's childhood palace became factories producing all manner of goods. The area served by the metro station Elektrozavodskaya (Electric Factory) is one such district. However, the streets have retained their quiet, nineteenth-century look even here, and there are a number of examples of the carved and embellished wooden houses that once were so common in Moscow. The factory owners, even when highly successful, preferred to live in or near the factory grounds. As they were attracted to the idiosyncratic style of Art Nouveau or a highly individual neo-baroque, it often happens that a dramatic house will be found nestling against a sober factory building. Next to one

such sinuously carved house of the Nosov textile manufacturers, is their earlier residence, unremarkable from the outside, but within harbouring surprising interiors added in the first decade of this century.

A little to the north-east is the great span of Sokolniki Park, once a hunting ground for the Tsars (sokol means falcon) and a favourite place for today's Muscovites who can relax or even ski in it throughout the winter. Much further eastwards, beyond the factory districts and almost to the Automobile Ring Road, there are a disconcerting number of old churches and other buildings, remnants of ancient villages which were swept away when the area was redeveloped in the 1960s and 70s. The most remarkable of these survivors is the huge estate at Kuskovo, built in what was then countryside by Pyotr Sheremetiev in the middle of the eighteenth century. The beautiful wooden palace and cottages and pavilions scattered throughout the garden – the grotto, Dutch House, Orangerie – are situated on the banks of a large artificial lake.

13C. Chertkov Mansion: the central White Hall forms part of the suite of reception rooms.

13D. Chertkov Mansion: the Gothic hall in the east wing.

· 13 ·

CHERTKOV MANSION

On Myasnitskaya (Kirov) Street, where it turns slightly north from Lubyanka (Dzerzhinsky) Square past the massive brooding building of the KGB, is a large old mansion set back in the shape of a 'u'. From the outside its once noble form is greatly in need of restoration, but the interior is one of the most singular in Moscow.

The history of the old mansion goes back to the time of Peter the Great when Tsarevich Kasimov, vassal of the Muscovy Tsars, lived here. In 1729 the powerful Dolgoruky family owned the mansion at the time of their fall from power during the reign of Anna Ivanovna. Later, it became the property of a hero of the Battle of Borodino, Major-General Saltykov. Exceptionally, the mansion did not burn in the great Moscow Fire of 1812 although it was heavily looted.

Its most interesting period is associated with the residence of the Marshal of the Nobility, Count A.D. Chertkov. An archeologist and avid bibliophile, he created what was then Moscow's largest private library (22,000 volumes) used by both Pushkin and Lev Tolstoy. The left wing of the house was built especially to contain the library in 1859 after which it was catalogued and opened to the public. (In 1872 it was given to the City of Moscow and is now in the History Library.)

In 1880 the house was purchased by a business woman, Obidina, who let the main rooms to various learned societies including the Moscow Architectural Society which sprang up in the city at this time. On the street in front of the house Obidina built some small shops, which have since been demolished.

The interior plasterwork, executed with rare panache, is most unusual. The oldest of the many reception rooms is the large 1844 Gothic hall with fine filigree mouldings. The white plaster fireplace in

13. Chertkov Mansion: E: a painting of Lenin reading ticker-tape on the principal staircase.
F: paint on plaster creates the illusion of leather in the Moorish smoking room.

the central White Hall, like the rest of the of the late nineteenth century, is the most astonishing. Cherubs, a nymph and satyr are tangled up in vines that twist and turn to the ceiling embracing a tall mirror. The effect is almost Gaudiesque, a wonderful fantasy, where the fireplace itself becomes irrelevant. Another curiosity is the small smoking room on the ground floor, decorated in the so-called 'Moorish' style in what seems to be leather but is in fact garishly painted plasterwork.

After the Revolution this curious building was taken over as the Businessmen's Club to train the new managers in the running of the economy. Later it became the House of Engineers and finally, in 1955, under the Znaniye (knowledge) Society, the Dzerzhinsky House of Scientific-Technical Propaganda, a kind of information service for science and new technology. Some of the Soviet Union's most respected scientists give lectures here. Thus, in a way, it has reverted to its pre-Revolutionary role as a meeting place for learned societies.

13G. *Chertkov Mansion: the plasterwork fireplace in the White Hall.*

·14·

BARYSHNIKOV MANSION

On Myasnitskaya (Kirov) Street opposite Le Corbusier's 1936 masterpiece — an office block with striking horizontal fenestration on the familiar *piloti* — is another stunning building, totally different in style and concept, the superb classical mansion built for the influential Baryshnikov family in 1797-1802 by Matvei Kazakov.

With fine proportions, set well back behind a driveway, the central portico is raised high on a rusticated basement. The low two-storey wings spread out to the street on either side of the main building form a *cours d'honneur*.

The left wing, the grander part of the house, has been recently restored. At its extreme end is the famous ballroom; although the room is almost square, the impression of an oval shape is given by the circular colonnade, within the quadrangle, of slim Corinthian columns in a rich, golden-sand colour, and by the similarly shaped ceiling painting. There is a lovely enfilade of rooms with fine bas-reliefs leading eventually to the main bedroom opposite the portico.

The house, which survived the 1812 Moscow Fire, belonged in the 1820s to Col. S.N. Begichev, son-in-law of the Baryshnikovs. The writer, society wit and diplomat Alexander Griboyedov, a close friend of the colonel, was a guest of the house in 1823-4 and while there completed his famous rhyming satirical comedy, *Woe from Wit*. He most likely read excerpts from his work while staying at the Baryshnikovs; the censors would not allow it to be published in his lifetime, but it became well known through private readings and circulation of the manuscript.

From the middle of the nineteenth century until the Revolution it was the Myasnitskaya Hospital; it then became the Research Institute of Sanitary Education. Stalin, who during the war worked in the staff headquarters building across the street, used part of the magnificent premises for his private cinema.

Another transformation took place

A

14. Baryshnikov Mansion: A: the stove and mouldings are typical of late eighteenth-century mansions.
B: a detail of the ceiling in the main bedroom.

B

14C. Baryshnikov Mansion: the ballroom with its beautiful oval ceiling.

when, in 1989, the popular weekly, *Argumenti i Fakti* (Arguments and Facts), took over the building. The controversial weekly, founded only eleven years ago, has had astonishing success with the advent of *glasnost*, as it set out to publish hitherto unknown or hidden facts and outspoken interviews about Soviet history, society and politics. Its circulation grew weekly to its present size of well over 30 million readers which has earned it a place in the *Guinness Book of Records*. Its popularity is such that in the spring of 1990 five members of the editorial staff were elected to the Russian parliament. *Argumenti i Fakti*'s outspokenness has frequently got it into trouble with the authorities and, as social critics, its journalists are not unworthy successors to that earlier tenant, Griboyedov.

· 15 ·

THE PERLOV TEA HOUSE

Among the dark greys, the dull ochres and prosaic exteriors of the commercial and business establishments on Myasnitskaya (Kirov) Street near its junction with the Boulevard is a most unusual building that appears to belong to another world. The façade is densely packed with delicate, lace-like carvings, pagoda roofs over every vertical bay and a three-tiered roof tower with upturned edges in place of a pediment. Every section is brightly coloured in reds, greens and golds with, on the ground floor, typography in pseudo-Chinese lettering announcing the sale of tea, coffee and cocoa.

The tea business was a lucrative one in Moscow at the end of the nineteenth century when it could be easily imported from China along the Trans-Siberian Railway. A rich merchant, A. Perlov, decided to erect a large office building with a shop on the ground floor in the desirable Myasnitskaya Street. In 1893 one of Moscow's best-known architects, Roman Klein, erected a large three-storey building. But Perlov was not satisfied with an ordinary office block and shop; he wanted the building to be instantly identifiable with his tea business. In 1895 the talented architect K.K. Gippius added the amazing pseudo-Chinese façade filling every inch of space of the building with Chinese ornamentation. There is a legend that it was so

15A. *Perlov Tea House: a detail of the biscuit and sweet counter.*

designed to impress the representative of the Manchu Dynasty in Moscow for the coronation of Nicholas II in 1896 and to divert his attention from the other tea merchants. As an advertising medium it was and is most successful; as an architectural device it looks grotesque and out of place on this street. Nevertheless, it adds a large dose of much-needed colour, especially considering its position opposite the grim grey post office.

The shop within on the ground floor is

unexpectedly narrow, with room only for a long aisle and counters and an island where the cashier with abacus and cash register reigns. It is even more richly adorned than the outside. The original shop furniture has survived intact; it is distinguished by dark, burnished reds relieved by gold and green ornamentation and here and there tall Chinese-like vases. The blue panelled ceiling makes it seem suffocating and lower than it actually is, a sort of pseudo-Chinese cavern.

15B. Perlov Tea House: dragons and other strange animals cavort about the counter stacked with tea.

The shop, which has the reputation of being better stocked than most Moscow stores, was originally set up to sell coffee, tea and cocoa; these days it also stocks cakes, biscuits and sweets when these items are available. It is, therefore, popular and always packed with determined, pushing crowds. In fact the wonderful interior must be lost to most members of the public who can only glimpse the ceiling and furniture through the throng.

· 16 ·

THE ALEKSEI MOROZOV
MANSION

The Aleksei Morozov Mansion is the largest house on Podsosensky (Under the Pines) Lane. It was built by M.N. Chichagov in 1879 for Vikuly Morozov of the famous Moscow merchant dynasty, Old Believers, who initially made their immense wealth in textile manufacture.

Aleksei Vikulovich, son of Vikuly, acquired an outstanding collection of porcelain and ceramics. After the Revolution, it was nationalized, but not initially removed from the house and Aleksei Vikulovich, who preferred not to abandon his precious porcelains for the attractions of the West, was allowed to go on living in his own house in two small rooms acting as curator to the newly established museum. However, by 1930, the great porcelain and ceramic collection was transferred to the eighteenth-century estate at Kuskovo where part of it is now displayed.

B

A

16. Aleksei Morozov Mansion: A: a gnome guards the stairs to the library.
B: the study with jasper fireplace and ceiling lighting panels.

If the façade of the Morozov Mansion is rather lugubrious, its bizarre interior is in striking contrast. Most of the first-floor reception rooms are by Chichagov in the rich, pastel-coloured baroque of the period, but they pale before the rooms on the ground floor executed some fifteen years later by Fyodor Shekhtel, responsible for some of the most arresting buildings in Moscow at the turn of the century, and closely associated with the large Morozov clan.

Shekhtel's suite of rooms to the left of the entrance that make up the hall and study of the master of the house are brilliantly designed in an imaginative neo-Gothic. The dark green ante-room with gold fleur-de-lys leads to an amazing hall which extends through two floors. The hall is dominated by the grotesque fireplace and staircase with the gnome perched at the bottom maliciously grinning, a book open at his feet on which is enscribed in Latin, 'Life is short, Art is eternal'. Off the hallway is the study decorated extravagantly in curvaceous baroque fashion with a richly red jasper fireplace and an interesting ceiling configuration which is really an ingenious lighting panel. Above the study, entered by the wooden staircase of the hallway, is the library, with original furniture including the dodecahedral table.

After the dispersal of the Morozov collection at the end of the 1920s, the mansion became first a students' club and later the editorial offices of the Academy of Sciences. The Academy is undertaking extensive restoration of both the Shekhtel and Chichagov rooms and, once they are complete, the great porcelain and ceramic collection at Kuskovo may return to its original home which would reopen as the Museum of Porcelain, a fitting compliment to the Morozov connection.

16C. Aleksei Morozov Mansion: the library with original table, cabinets and frieze.

17A. Kazan Railway Station: the highly decorated ceiling of the restaurant overwhelms the diners.

· 17 ·

THE KAZAN RAILWAY
STATION

Lively Komsomol Square boasts three railway stations in three completely opposing styles: the classical Leningrad, the Yaroslavl in Art Nouveau and the Kazan, a romantic essay on the Russian past. Of the three, the Kazan, which carries traffic to Central Asia, Siberia and the Urals, is the largest with the longest front, an amalgamation of different heights and shapes taken from existing medieval Russian buildings and combined in one great picturesque array.

Construction of the unusual station began in 1913 to the design of the architect, Aleksei Shchusev, whose task was to build a 'Gateway to the East'. The intervention of the First World War followed by the upheavals of the Revolution delayed its completion until 1926. The career of Shchusev, the most Soviet of architects, was so well established before the Revolution that he was given this project and the enormous sum of 3 million gold rubles to spend on it. Shchusev had been deeply impressed by the psuedo-Russian style of the Igumnov House and Vasnetsov's neo-Russian façade of the Tretyakov Gallery and took easily recognizable models for the various sections of the station exterior which he then joined together. Part of his concept, however, to

advertise the beauties of Moscow baroque, was lost in 1940 when it was decided to reface the brick façade in the ubiquitous marble so beloved of the leadership in the Stalin era.

The interior relates superficially to the grand architecture of the façade which is like the wall of a medieval city. This medieval motif is not entirely forgotten, but is of less importance in the gigantic waiting hall with its high ceiling where the vaulting and window frames are those of the sixteenth century. However, it is a railway station after all, built in the twentieth century of reinforced concrete, to accommodate noisy, modern machines.

The most splendid part of the interior is surely the restaurant with its high-vaulted ceiling dwarfing the diners below. The

B

C

richly moulded décor is especially evident in the ceiling where paintings have been placed inside elaborate scrolls. The colour scheme is most effective; the light green of the walls contrasted with the dark blue background of the ceiling. It comes as no surprise to discover that the restaurant's paintings are by the same artist, Yevgeny Lansere, who later did the mosaic panels in the Komsomolskaya metro station, which links all three railway stations.

Recently the station has been modernized to increase its capacity four-fold. A glass canopy which doubles as a passage-way has been erected over the platforms and links the new buildings to the old hall. Happily, the architecture of the old building will be entirely preserved.

17. Kazan Railway Station: B: the crowds seem miniscule in the capacious waiting-room. C: a detail of a fresco.

· 18 ·

THE CHURCH OF THE
ARCHANGEL GABRIEL

On a pleasant lane near Chistoprudny (clean pond) Boulevard is the Church of the Archangel Gabriel popularly known as the Menshikov Tower. One of the most distinctive buildings in Moscow, its red walls with white details rise in succeeding octagonal tiers, tall, impressive and visible, even in today's cramped Moscow, from unexpected vantage points.

The church was commissioned as the chapel of his considerable mansion by Alexander Menshikov, who rose from obscure origins to become the most power-ful man in Russia under Peter the Great with the titles of Prince, Senator and Field Marshal. Menshikov, in emulation of Peter, wanted a new type of church closer to western fashions and chose the sculptor Ivan Zarudny as architect. The church was erected in 1704-7 in the form of a tower, the cube base surmounted by three octagons which accommodated the bell-tower, the uppermost one bearing an En-glish musical clock. The tower culminated in a spire and the figure of an angel and cross. When completed it was the tallest building in Moscow, taller even than the Ivan Veliky bell-tower in the Kremlin, but its supremacy was short-lived; the topmost of the three octagonal tiers was destroyed by lightning in 1723. It was only in the 1770s that the church was repaired, but the top tier and the spire were not replaced and the open arches where the bells had hung were filled in. The whole was crowned with a dome and gold finial. Now modestly lower than the Kremlin bell-tower, it became known as the 'bride of Ivan Veliky'.

The Menshikov Tower introduced new baroque features into Moscow archi-tecture. The Russian Orthodox Church still did not sanction three dimensional forms, but with the growing influence of baroque, sculptural embellishments such as those of the Menshikov Tower, both inside and out, were tolerated.

Inside the church, although not all of the original work has survived, the preoccupa-tion with sculptural forms is obvious. There is a wealth of plaster decoration in figures of angels, cartouches, garlands of fruit and flowers. The nineteenth-century

18A. Archangel Gabriel: sculptural ornamentation was an unusual innovation in this church.

iconostasis was brought here in 1968 when the Church of the Transfiguration in eastern Moscow was pulled down.

A curious historical fact about the church is that after it suffered from a fire in 1723 and lay in ruins for fifty years, it was restored by the influential group of Moscow Masons who happened to have their lodge in a nearby lane. In the second half of the eighteenth century the masonic movement, brought to Russia by an Englishman, was very popular among the aristocracy for whom it became a secret debating club of free-thinkers. Having repaired the church the Masons used it for their own rituals and decorated the interior with their symbols.

At the beginning of the nineteenth century, the church, which began its life as the domestic chapel of a prince, became the humble post office chapel. This is because Menshikov's large mansion was taken over at about that time by the post office as its main building in Moscow (rebuilt in 1912). It retained its post office association until after the Revolution.

· 19 ·

THE CHURCH OF ST FYODOR STRATILATUS

Next to the Menshikov Tower and closely associated with it is another church, the elegant St Fyodor Stratilatus, built in 1806 for the post office by the well-known classical architect, I.V. Yegotov. It provides the bell-tower which the Menshikov Tower has lacked since 1723. On top of its roof in place of the normal cupola or dome is a charming open belfry. The church originally had a grand portico of Corinthian columns and pediment facing the street, but it was stripped off in Soviet times to allow passage along the pavement. It is much broader and more spacious inside than most of Moscow's churches for it lacks the usual aisles or a *trapeznaya* (ante-room).

These two churches, the Church of the Archangel Gabriel and the Church of St Fyodor Stratilatus, create an island of religion in a district of Moscow otherwise

18B. Archangel Gabriel: the ornate, nineteenth-century iconostasis was rescued from a demolished church.

19A. St Fyodor: a side chapel set within a niche.

19B. St Fyodor: the unusual lack of aisles provides a sense of space.

bare of functioning churches. They contrast in style – one representing the first brave use of western baroque in the city, the other the more restrained and conventional classical approach. The bells of St Fyodor, for long silenced after the Revolution, were heard again in 1989 calling the faithful to service. They start with a curious dissonant sound, at first ponderous and slow, gradually gathering momentum until all the bells are involved and a joyous and compelling peal can be heard all over the district from the Boulevards to the Lubyanka. The two churches are now used by the mission of the Greek Orthodox Patriarchate of Antioch and All the East, but services are conducted in Russian according to the rites of the Russian Orthodox Church.

· 20 ·

THE THEATRE OF HISTORY

On the initiative of a group of theatrical artists directed by Nikolai Zelenetsky and inspired by Madame Tussaud's, a wax museum of historical figures from Russian history has been created in one of Moscow's main parks, Sokolniki. Here, among the avenues that fan out from the centre of the former hunting park, a huge hand outside a small flat-roofed pavilion points the way to the entrance.

Inside the dark passage the only light emanates from the tableaux in which various Russian historical personalities are

depicted. The dominant theme is the propensity of autocrats to stifle the free expression of art and culture. It is the first time in modern Russia that life-size models have been used to make critical political and historical statements. It is a consequence of the freedom of speech that has grown under the policy of *glasnost* to embrace every shade of opinion. Huge crowds flock here at weekends to be titillated by the sight of formerly awesome leaders in curious juxtapositions.

There are only fifteen figures in all. Beyond the huge hand holding the hour glass, they include Ivan the Terrible with Pushkin and Stalin in the first group. Most striking of all is the scene where Nicholas II with a hole through his head is watching a game of chess. One of the players is

20. Theatre of History: a tableau of Stalin and Ivan the Terrible with Pushkin.

Malyuta Skuratov, the notorious commander of the *oprichniki*, the private army of Ivan the Terrible, which terrorized the people. Among Skuratov's many crimes was the murder of Metropolitan Philip who dared to stand up against the Tsar. The other player is Lavrenty Beria in familiar pince-nez, Stalin's most notorious henchman, and head of the secret police in the last decade of Stalin's reign. They are easily two of the most despicable characters in Russian history. Stalin liked to compare himself with Ivan the Terrible whom he evidently considered a stern, but wise, leader surrounded by enemies and misunderstood. Eisenstein's classic film *Ivan the Terrible* made during the war years (under close supervision by Stalin) testifies to this interpretation.

In another tableau the late Leonid Brezhnev, renowned for his indolence, is reclining in an armchair behind which the ballad singer and famous actor Vladimir Vysotsky strums his guitar. Vysotsky wrote satirical and subversive ballads on many subjects and died tragically young in 1980. Tens of thousands of Muscovites joined the funeral procession from the Taganka Theatre where he worked, and his grave in the Vagankovsky Cemetery has become a shrine. The ballet dancer, Maya Plisetskaya (the only living person represented), stands by herself gracefully pirouetting. Probably in the future the display will include more contemporary political figures.

· 21 ·

KUSKOVO

East of the central part of Moscow beyond the Old Believers' community at Rogozhskoe and past glum factory districts is Kuskovo, the ideal eighteenth-century estate, with formal garden, church, main house, cottages, pond and grotto. The country house of the fabulously wealthy Counts Sheremetiev from the early seventeenth century until 1917, its quiet opulence has survived almost in its entirety the French invasion and the upheavals of Revolution.

Kuskovo was built for Pyotr Shere-

metiev, the son of Field Marshal Boris Sheremetiev, Peter the Great's closest military commander. A number of architects, craftsmen and master builders worked at the estate over forty years, 1740-80. Some of the Count's own serfs were educated as architects and three played a major role in the arrangement of Kuskovo – Aleksei Mironov, Fyodor Argunov and Grigory Dikushin. The façade of the main house was commissioned from the French architect Charles de Wailly (designer of the Odéon in Paris), but the serf-architect, Argunov, did the actual construction supervised by the Moscow architect, Karl Blank.

The main palace built of wood with a stone foundation was meant to be used as a

summer retreat; the Sheremetievs liked to spend the month of June there. Of one floor only, it is not grand in the sense of the huge royal palaces which were erected about the same time near St Petersburg. It is in the early classical style with a driveway flanked by two sphynxes. The noblest room is the rectangular ballroom with a wonderful ceiling painting of Apollo on a cloud representing the glory of the Sheremetievs.

The domed grotto entered by fine wrought-iron gates was built in 1756-71 by Argunov and decorated inside with shells of all sorts and sizes designed by Johannes Fokt, the St Petersburg 'Master of Grotto work'. It is spacious and cool inside, a delightful hideaway on a hot summer's day.

21C. Kuskovo: the crimson drawing-room with portraits of Count Pyotr Sheremetiev and the Empress Elizabeth.

In 1812 the French occupied the house and inflicted much damage, shooting holes in the paintings of the Sheremetiev ancestors and damaging the tapestries. Dmitry Sheremetiev, grandson of Pyotr, refused to allow the portraits to be repaired because he wanted to be reminded of the occupation of the French; it was only when Soviet supremacy was established that they were restored.

Pyotr's son, Nikolai, did not like Kuskovo, preferring the estate he built at Ostankino for his bride, Praskovia Zhemchugova, the serf-actress. Kuskovo was

D

E

21. Kuskovo: D: the formal entrance hall of the main palace. E: the second drawing-room with original tapestries and ornamental stove. F: a grand tea is laid out in the sunny east room.

F

21G. Kuskovo: the long ballroom with ceiling painted by Lagrenée the Elder.

little used in the nineteenth century although it was the custom to open the grounds to the public twice a week right up to the Revolution. It was nationalized in 1919 and in 1932 the Morozov porcelain collection was moved to the Orangerie and it became the Museum of Ceramics. The park and the large pond for bathing and boating in the summer make it a delightful spot for Muscovites to relax in.

· 22 ·

THE MEDIEVAL HOUSE OF THE YUSUPOVS

On a quiet lane in the old part of Moscow is a late seventeenth-century house coloured a rich red with striking white con-

trasts and saturated in the architectural detail typical of Moscow baroque. Built in sections of varying heights, each with its own steeply pitched chequer-board roof, pendules and intricate window frames, it is joined together by the exterior wall.

At the beginning of the eighteenth century, it was inhabited by Peter Tolstoy who, as head of the Secret Chancellery, persuaded the recalcitrant Tsarevich,

22A. Yusupov House: *florid nineteenth-century design imitates an earlier style.*

Alexei, Peter the Great's ill-fated son, to come back to Russia from Austria. The wretched youth who had no political ambition was promptly incarcerated and eventually died after prolonged torture, probably with the connivance of his father.

In 1727 the distinguished Yusupov family, descendants of the Nogai Khans, were granted the palace when the previous owner fell from grace. The Yusupovs rarely used the Moscow property, letting it in their absence to other members of the aristocracy; Russia's greatest poet, Pushkin, lived there as a child. The Yusupovs held it for nearly two centuries until they were forced to leave Russia after the Revolution; the family name achieved notoriety in 1916 when the young Felix Yusupov succeeded, after several attempts, in murdering the notorious Rasputin regarded as an evil influence on Empress Alexandra.

Inside, it is a warren of offices and passages that go up and down and around making the casual visitor quite dizzy; the original organization of the house has not been altered and the different sections are joined by narrow corridors. The interior décor of the house is an imaginative recreation of how it might have been in the seventeenth century. The same artists and architects who were busy 'restoring' the Kremlin palaces were also engaged to renew Yusupov House. Thus the architect, N. V. Sultanov, 'restored' the east wing during 1892-5 adding the colourful enclosed porch and the walls and gates bearing the Yusupov family crest. F.G. Solntsev repainted the interior throughout 1860-70. However, the highly decorative wall paintings which cover even the vaulted ceilings are deeply impressive in their own right. The Krestovy or Cross Hall, the magnificent main reception room of the house, is unaltered in form, a large vaulted room without pillar or columns, 14 metres in each direction.

The present tenants, the Academy of Agricultural Sciences, who have been there for many decades, are proud to have such singular offices, low vaulted ceilings richly painted in dark blues and reds and outlined in gold, staircases in unexpected places, splendid tiled stoves in the corners and the great gold Yusupov lion holding in his paws the crest of the ancient family.

....

22B. Yusupov House: one of the colourful tiled stoves in the old part of the house.

22C. *Yusupov House: the gold lion displays the Yusupov family crest.*

A

23A and B: Nosov House: the corners of the vaulted ceiling are the heads of the gods.

· 23 ·

THE NOSOV HOUSE

In the unlikely setting of an industrial district in east Moscow near the Elektrozavodskaya metro (Electric Factory) are a number of charming old mansions, some in vivacious Art Nouveau, others more placidly classical in style. One such was the home of the Nosovs, textile barons of the last century.

The Nosov House looks unpretentious from outside, an irregular two-storey house of the 1880s with large windows and the entrance from the courtyard. It looks onto the square where in 1902 a People's House, a sort of cultural centre, was built by the city architect, Ivanov-Shits.

Yerofimiya Pavlovna, the vivacious and attractive daughter of the banker, magnate and politician, Pavel Ryabushinsky, married V.V. Nosov and came to live in this house. She was keenly interested in contemporary art and collected the paintings of leading Russian artists with the intention of leaving them all to the city of Moscow as Pavel Tretyakov had done with his unique collection. She wanted her house to be suitable as an art gallery and, with this in mind, invited the 'Palladian' architect, Ivan Zholtovsky, who had immersed himself in Italian architecture, to redesign the principal room, the Hall of Columns, in the majestic style of the neoclassical. This he did most successfully during 1907-8.

In 1912-13 Yerofimiya invited the theatre artist, Mstislav Dobuzhinsky, to decorate the main stairwell, and link it with the Hall of Columns and the dining-room with suitably impressive paintings. The resulting dramatic gold ceiling, which looks like mosaic, was done in a classical theme on a cobalt blue background.

After the Revolution like many other merchants' houses the Nosov House was nationalized. With its fine collection of paintings, it made the transition to the local Museum of the Proletariat. For a short period it was a nursery school before it became a workers' Palace of Culture at the end of the 1920s. The building did not suffer unduly until 1935 when it became a local House (Club) of Komsomol and Schoolchildren. At this time new doors were cut into the house,

windows added and others closed up, and much of the interior décor lost. But, in 1949, an enterprising local teacher with the help of his pupils began the task of setting up a museum of the history of the district. They searched for photographs and artifacts of past years and succeeded at last in 1962 in opening the local museum of Pervomaisky Rayon (first of any district) in the old Nosov House. When in 1980 it was decided to restore the house the old photographs collected by the children were a great help. Thus the main room, the Hall of Columns, the landing of the main staircase with Dobuzhinsky's astonishing ceiling, and the dining-room were fully restored.

· 24 ·

METRO KOMSOMOLSKAYA

The three main railway stations situated on Komsomol Square are linked to central Moscow through the metro station, Komsomolskaya. This was part of the first line, the Kirovo-Frunzenskaya, opened with much fanfare in 1935. Its two vestibules provide access to and from the Leningrad and Yaroslavl Stations on the north side of the square, and from the Kazan Station on the south side. The station's simple design of powerful rose-coloured marble columns includes large majolica panels by Yevgeny Lansere, the artist of the Kazan Railway Station restaurant above. The panels depict heroic metro workers, many of them volunteer members of the Komsomol (Young Communist League) constructing the underground railway.

The second line on Komsomolskaya, the Circle, was opened in 1952, nearly twenty years later, and the evolution of the palatial underground style as it developed from the early Stalin period to the end of the era (he was to die a year later) could not be more obvious than by comparing the two parts of the station. The architect was Aleksei Shchusev, who had designed the flamboyant Kazan Railway Station and was the leading Soviet architect. He responded wholeheartedly to the change in fashion moving away from the simpler,

24. Metro Komsomolskaya: the mosaic illustrates the annual celebration of the revolution in Red Square.

more restrained early metro stations, towards elaborate and rich decoration. The
northern vestibule of the earlier line was
altered and enlarged for the new line of
1952, making it the most spacious of
Moscow's metro stations to accommodate
the vast number of people arriving daily in
Moscow via the three railways.

It was also the most richly decorated.
For people coming into Moscow from the
country for the first time the richness of the
décor must be overwhelming. Ceiling cartouches contain panels in the ubiquitous
mosaic, with gold as the dominant colour,
designed by Pavel Korin, the portraitist
and 'monumentalist' and also the artist of
the metro stations Novoslobodskaya and
Smolenskaya, who had to suppress his
profoundly religious feelings during the
Stalin period. The mosaics display subjects
which had become kitsch and banal: the
taking of the Reichstag; Victory; the 7
November military parade in Red Square
in 1941; and a host of famous generals
from Russian history. In keeping with
changes in the Soviet leadership the group
shown watching the Red Square parade
has undergone diverting alterations; in the
course of the 1950s Beria and Stalin were
erased from the leaders standing on the
tribune and finally Khrushchev disappeared after his dismissal in 1964.

· 25 ·

METRO TAGANSKAYA

The metro station Taganskaya, on the east
side of the highly decorative Circle Line,
was opened in 1950, the first of the three
lines which meet here. The theme of the
'Great Patriotic War' as the Russians call
the Second World War which distinguishes
many of the stations on the Circle Line is
evident in the décor of the main hall.
Inside, depicted on elaborate blue ceramic
triangular frames between each marble
archway leading to the platforms are bas-
relief medallions of the 'defenders of the
motherland' – pilots, tank drivers, infan-
try, partisans. Taganskaya links up with
two radial lines, a second Taganskaya
opened in 1966 and Marksistskaya in
1979.

*25. Metro Taganskaya: the bas-relief of a Soviet
soldier of the Second World War.*

One amazing feature of the Moscow underground system is that however far one travels or however many times one changes line, the price remained the same – 5 copecks – the price charged when the metro was first opened over fifty years ago. Indeed, the ticket was the 5 copeck coin itself, a most efficient and simple method. At the present rate of exchange 5 copecks is half an English penny; it is more realistic to compare it to 5 pence. With the desire to introduce cost accounting into the Soviet system the price of the metro was finally increased in April 1991 to 15 copecks which, although three times more, is still inexpensive. The train service is fast and efficient, trains arrive within the minute in rush hour and about three minutes otherwise. With the cheap price, fast service, clean, palatial station halls, underground travel in Moscow is probably the best value in Europe.

· 26 ·

ELISO VIRSALADZE

The pianist, Eliso Virsaladze, is a well-known soloist, a Merited Artist of the USSR, who is also a teacher at the Conservatory. She is a Georgian and studied at the Tbilisi Conservatory where her grandmother, Anastasia Virsaladze, was one of her teachers. Her success was assured when she won third prize in the piano section of the important Tchaikovsky Competition in 1962 – the exceptional year when Vladimir Ashkenazy and Britain's John Ogdon tied for first place. In the Tchaikovsky piano competition of 1990 her pupil, Boris Berezovsky (who had taken fourth prize at the Leeds piano festival in 1987), won first prize and another of her pupils, James Kirby from Britain, gave an excellent performance.

Eliso Virsaladze has become very well known as a concert pianist abroad, particularly in Germany where her repertoire of Mozart, Beethoven, Schumann and Brahms is greatly appreciated. She also tours other countries including, in the autumn of 1990, Britain. She has played in a trio with Natalia Gutman (cello) and Oleg Kagan (violin) who sadly died recently. She sometimes plays with the Borodin Quartet, the best-known string quartet in the Soviet Union, with whom she travels extensively throughout the world.

Eliso lives with her daughter and husband near a large park in the Sokolniki district, named for the royal falconers of the seventeenth century, in an ordinary Moscow flat into which, somehow, she manages to squeeze two pianos.

26. Eliso Virsaladze: the pianist and teacher.

28A. Moscow Arts Theatre: the carefully restored foyer showing Shekhtel's decorative squares.

NORTH MOSCOW

Moscow's lovely central squares were grafted on to the radial-concentric pattern of the city after the disastrous Fire of 1812 when Napoleon briefly occupied Moscow. Within this area perhaps the most successful of these squares was constructed, known as Theatre Square, although for seventy-two years it was called Sverdlov after the Bolshevik leader. It was built as a large rectangular space, bigger than the Place de la Concorde in Paris. Surrounded by classical buildings, among which the Bolshoi Theatre dominated, it contained a bare parade ground in its centre. The troublesome Neglinnaya River, which ran along the west wall of the Kremlin and Kitai-Gorod and turned north through the square, was placed in conduits underground in 1817-19, thus freeing more space.

The Maly Theatre to the right of the Bolshoi is one of the few classical buildings that has survived. The Bolshoi, designed by Andrei Mikhailov in 1825 in place of the ruined Petrov Theatre, suffered badly from a fire in 1853 and was rebuilt less successfully by Albert Cavos. A garden with fountains is laid out in front of the theatre screening it from the twelve lanes of heavy traffic which now bisect the square. On the other side of this noisy road the splendidly restored Metropole Hotel, built at the beginning of the century in Art Nouveau style, takes up one quarter of the square.

Beyond the Bolshoi streets fan out north and east and are sliced by others in curving, concentric rings. This old part of Moscow includes the main pre-Revolutionary shopping street Kuznetsky Most, or Smith's Bridge, named after the former bridge that spanned the Neglinnaya before it disappeared underground. The bridge still exists under the road and there is a plan to expose it again. Kuznetsky Most is still a very busy street full of small shops selling books, clothing and music. Nearby is the neo-Gothic former department store, Muir and Mirrielees, founded by two Scots before the Revolution and rebuilt in the Soviet period as TsUM. Cars can hardly get through these small streets and they are already largely pedestrian zones.

Unusually for Moscow, the steep banks of the Neglinnaya

35A. Metropole Hotel: a motif.

provide some relief in the flat city and attractive lanes rise up on each side of the wide river. There are two famous steam baths near the river, the Tsentralny and the Sandunovsky. Steam baths to this day are part of the Russian way of life.

Further over to the east is Lubyanka (Dzerzhinsky) Square with the great building of the Lubyanka brooding over it. The headquarters of the KGB with its basement prisons is no longer so fearsome; in the not-so-distant past it was the main centre to which people were brought for interrogation before either being shot or exiled to Siberia. The KGB use many buildings in the nearby streets; nearly all the houses on B. Lubyanka (Dzerzhinsky) Street, including the famous mansion of the Governor of Moscow, during the Napoleonic invasion, Rostopchin, belong to them.

Although many churches have been demolished since the Revolution in this central part of Moscow, a large number survive, including the glorious Upper Peter Monastery on the Petrovka with its red and white Moscow baroque style. It is now used by the Ministry of Culture and is undergoing lengthy restoration, although for a long time all the buildings, even the bell-tower, were divided into crowded flats. The Convent of the Nativity, too, is located in this quarter on the Neglinnaya bank with its ancient cathedral of about 1500, one of the oldest churches in Moscow (no longer functioning). Beyond, the quiet tree-lined Boulevards erected in the early nineteenth century in place of the walls of Bely Gorod encircle Moscow, providing a much needed, if somewhat narrow, green belt. Another short Boulevard runs at right angles to the main one on the site of the river, the Tsvetnoi or Flower Boulevard, where the Central Market and Old Circus are to be found.

The area includes Tverskaya (Gorky) Street, Moscow's main thoroughfare which, despite intensive rebuilding in the 1930s and 40s, contains some fascinating buildings. One such is the food shop formerly known as Yeliseyev's that has somehow managed to preserve its 1901 interior and even the original furniture.

There are many theatres in this part of Moscow. Apart from the Bolshoi perhaps the most interesting are the Moscow Arts Theatre with its memories of Stanislavsky (there is a fascinating museum next door) and the innovative Komsomol Theatre on Chekhov Street which was built as the Merchants' Club. Its interior is in excellent condition and the Moscow Arts Theatre has just been thoroughly restored and refurbished.

Further out the busy Garden Ring Road, originally earthen ramparts, encircles the city, its gardens removed by the dictate of Stalin. Outside the Garden Ring there are a few functioning churches among the acres of tower blocks built from the late 1950s onward to try to solve the problem of accommodation for the ever-increasing population of Moscow. They encroach on former country areas, surrounding and dwarfing such estates as Ostankino, the lovely wooden palace built by Count Sheremetiev for his mistress, the serf-actress Praskovia Zhemchugova. The unexpected beauty of the palace is a tonic in the welter of drab housing. Its former grounds are now used for the grandiose Exhibition of Economic Achievements with its outmoded self-congratulatory ethos.

27. Chemist Shop: the original Art Nouveau furniture is still in situ.

28B. Moscow Arts Theatre: good typography identifies the dress circle.

· 27 ·

THE CHEMIST SHOP, 40 GORKY STREET

One of the substantial apartment buildings built at the beginning of the twentieth century on Tverskaya Yamskaya (Gorky) Street still has, as it did when it first opened, a small, busy chemist or apothecary shop. It is entered by a cheerless wooden door that slams loudly with the constant comings and goings of the many customers. Russians are obsessed with problems of health to the point where one suspects an element of hypochondria (not surprisingly given their heavy meat and bread diet and the lack of fresh vegetables in winter).

The goods on display and easily available at the chemist's are extremely cheap and many look old-fashioned and strange to the eye of a visitor. They include outdated (although often effective) remedies such as mustard plasters of the sort one's grandparents may have used and the curious little jam-jars for 'cupping', a procedure that even the most educated Russians seem to believe in. The patient, suffering from a severe cold, has his back covered with rows of these little jars. A vacuum is first obtained by burning a wad of cotton wool inside the jar and quickly placing it on the patient's back before oxygen has time to enter. The effect is to draw up the skin into the jars which somehow cures the condition. Leeches are still widely used for the treatment of high blood pressure.

This chemist shop, in spite of its limited and odd range of medicines and unimaginative display of goods, presents an attractive face. Through the door one is struck by the sheen of rich mahogany with bright ceramic mosaics that contrast with the dark wood. The entire length of the narrow shop is fitted out with the richly carved furniture that must have been especially designed for the original chemist shop in about 1900. Amazingly, all the fixtures seem to have survived – the mahogany display chest, curved and bowed, with the coloured ceramic inset. The staff in this shop are exceptionally helpful and pleasant; perhaps it comes from pride in the knowledge that they work in the most beautiful chemist/apothecary shop in Moscow.

· 28 ·

THE MOSCOW ARTS THEATRE

The famous Moscow Arts Company created by the arch-realist Konstantin Stanislavsky and his partner Nemirovich-Danchenko, found permanent refuge in the old Lianozov Theatre in 1902. In the surprisingly short period of four months Fyodor Shekhtel redesigned the interior to the latest canons: the stage was a revolving one, reasonably sized dressing rooms were provided, and the lighting, installed with the help of their wealthy patron, Savva Morozov, was centrally controlled, a remarkable innovation for the time.

Shekhtel's genius for interior design was admirably suited to respond to Stanislavsky's express plea that there be no frills and furbelows and the hall be plain and unadorned. The eye should not be distracted but entirely focused on the stage. Thus this theatre contrasts greatly with other Moscow theatres of the period with their ornate interiors. Here even the chairs of Finnish lime are plain and not heavily upholstered, discouraging any inclination to doze.

The original interior has been fully restored. Bands of Shekhtel's geometric squares enliven the plain expanse of wall. Signs in the fashionable lettering of that period request patrons to refrain from entering during performances and suggest that ladies remove their hats. The smoking and tea rooms are decorated with elegant ceilings of stem-like curving lines that end in flowers.

In its early years the Moscow Arts Theatre (MKhAT) was closely associated with Chekhov. *The Cherry Orchard*, a revolutionary play for its time, was first performed here with Olga Knipper, Chekhov's wife, in the leading role of Ranevskaya. Chekhov himself was present at the première in 1904, only a few months before he died so tragically of tuberculosis. Knipper, who survived Chekhov by fifty-five years, continued to perform at the MKhAT until she retired.

After the Revolution, Stanislavsky continued to seek new and interesting plays but he became more and more dictatorial and egotistical. His relationship with his co-director, Vladimir Nemirovich-Danchenko, became severely strained and the theatre operated under increasing tensions caricatured by the brilliant Russian writer, Mikhail Bulgakov, in his novel, *Black Snow*. Stanislavsky's death, and controls imposed in the Stalin and post-Stalin period, led to long dull years in which the theatre stagnated.

During restoration of the building the Arts Theatre, which had been using a new theatre on Tverskoi Boulevard, underwent an internal crisis finally resolved by the division of the company into two; the more avant-garde actors under Oleg Yefremov moved back into the original refurbished building, and the more conservative ele-

ments under the actress Tatyana Doronina remained in the new building, renamed the Theatre of the Friendship of the Peoples. Thus the Moscow Arts Theatre has been renewed not only physically by improvements in the building, but also artistically by the lifting of bureaucratic controls. Stanislavsky would have approved.

· 29 ·

YELISEYEV'S FOOD HALL

Gastronom No. 1 on Tverskaya (Gorky) Street has a most intriguing history. As the fine mansion in the 1820s of Zinaida Volkonskaya it was immensely suitable for her famous literary evenings. Something of a writer herself, she favoured the fashionable literary establishment and deeply admired Russia's foremost poet, the young Alexander Pushkin, who came to her soirées whenever he was in Moscow.

In December 1825, a group of young officers had attempted to stage an uprising against the new Tsar, Nicholas I, on Senate Square in St Petersburg. Known as the Decembrists, five were hanged, the rest, including members of some of the most illustrious noble families, were exiled in perpetuity to Siberia. In January 1827, Princess Maria, the wife of one of the leading Decembrists, Prince Sergei Volkonsky, and sister-in-law to Zinaida, came to bid farewell to Moscow, and her former life of ease. Pushkin was present on this notable and poignant occasion. Princess Maria was preparing to set out for eastern Siberia in the deep cold of winter thousands of miles away to share her husband's exile. This pampered woman was not to return to European Russia for thirty years. Pushkin was probably in love with her. He was silent and preoccupied all evening and a few days later sent her warm greetings and the famous poem dedicated to his friends in Siberia:

In the depths of the Siberian mines
preserve proud patience;
your grievous toil
and the high striving of your thoughts
will not be in vain.

28C. Moscow Arts Theatre: muted colours and good lighting focus attention on the stage.

29. *Yeliseyev's Food Hall: heavy ornate furniture and fittings still distinguish the food shop.*

The old mansion of Zinaida Volkonskaya was completely rebuilt in 1898-1901 by G.G. Yeliseyev as a luxurious emporium using only the shell and foundations of the old house. Yeliseyev, who owned a similar shop in St Petersburg, opened the most exclusive and expensive food shop in Moscow with a wildly extravagant décor that makes Harrods' Food Hall seem a model of restraint. Today the goods on display in Gastronom No. 1 do not resemble the variety and delicacies even of eighty years ago, and certainly not the Harrods of today.

Open seven days a week, it is always so crowded with aggressive, pushing customers that it is hard to make one's way inside and even harder to admire the wonderfully flamboyant interior. A plan is afoot to return Yeliseyev's to private ownership in an effort to solve the perennial Soviet problem of poor service and empty shelves.

····································

· 30 ·

····································

THE TSENTRALNY RESTAURANT

····································

In a prominent position on Tverskaya (Gorky) Street, the Tsentralny (Central) Restaurant attracts more customers than it can handle. A permanent queue seems always to collect at its entrance although a sign, all too familiar in Moscow, clearly indicates that there are no places. Once past the hostile doorman the restaurant does not seem all that crowded. Its richly sculptured décor and private, panelled cubicles make it one of Moscow's most pleasant restaurants.

The restaurant originated as a fashionable coffee house opened in 1905 by the wealthy baker, Filippov — indeed bread is still baked and sold on the premises. Two well-known artists, Pyotr Konchalovsky and Sergei Konenkov, contributed to the ornate interior decorations. In the process of building, relations between the bakery workers and the management worsened and, in common with many other Moscow workers, they went on strike. Cossacks sent to quell the disturbances were met by a barrage of bricks lying conveniently at hand by the unfinished building. The bakers were defeated, however, by the arrival of reinforcements who fired into

30A. Tsentralny Restaurant: the tables are ready to receive the diners.

the strikers, many of whom managed to flee into the neighbouring courtyards.

Those courtyards were to be used in another context some decades later. Next to the coffee house, in 1911, the Filippov family built a hotel known as the Luxe (the Tsentralnaya). In 1920, after the Revolution, the hotel became a hostel for delegates to meetings of the Communist International and for foreign communists whose population in the 1930s increased considerably with the rise of Hitler in Germany and right-wing governments elsewhere. The German, Bulgarian, Yugoslav, Italian and, above all, Polish Communists could not have imagined that life in the Soviet Union would become

more dangerous than at home; most of them became victims of the arrests and executions of the 30s. They were arrested at night, bundled out through the kitchens of the restaurant into the vehicles of the secret police and sped away to the nearby Lubyanka. The unhappy wives and children were moved to a less desirable block at the back of the hotel; they could only live by selling their belongings. Eventually they, too, were arrested and sent to the *gulag*, their children dispersed among the camps for children of 'enemies of the people'.

Tito, the Yugoslav leader, recalls living in the hotel in the summer of 1938 with the fear of arrest hanging over him. Sir Fitzroy

30B. Tsentralny Restaurant: a caryatid.

Maclean, in his book *Disputed Barricade*, remembers Tito eating with a fellow Yugoslav, Vlahovic, in the restaurant of the Luxe (the Tsentralny). Vlahovic remarked to Tito that no one would sit at their table. Tito, with amazing confidence, replied, 'It's of no importance, one day they will be falling over each others' chairs to sit with us.' However, as soon as he could, Tito returned to the safer perils of Yugoslavia, perhaps already determined on Yugoslavia's independent course.

· 31 ·

THE NATIONAL HOTEL

The National, in an enviable central position overlooking the Kremlin and Red Square, is one of Moscow's oldest and best hotels. Completed in 1901, it is a product of the great building boom that overtook Moscow at the end of the nineteenth century. Although less revolutionary in design than the Metropole Hotel built almost at the same time, the National contains

A

echoes of the then popular Art Nouveau style, particularly in its interior décor. It was designed by A.I. Ivanov in the freely interpreted classical style of the time. It is divided into horizontal bands – large windows on the rusticated first two floors, where the restaurants are located, then three floors of pilasters and elaborate windows containing the main rooms. On the corner, a ceramic roof panel of chimneys and factories replaced the original pastoral scene.

The National has been promoted to No. 1 Tverskaya (Gorky) Street with the demolition of all the buildings between it and the Kremlin. One that fell prey to the bulldozer which stood next to the hotel was the Victorian-looking Chapel of Alexander Nevsky built by public donation in 1888 by D. Chichagov to commemorate the liberation of the Bulgarians, with the help of Russian troops, from the Ottoman Empire.

The National, resplendent now in isolation, was designated the First House of the Soviets after the Revolution and its rooms became apartments for the new Soviet leaders. When the new Government moved to Moscow from Petrograd (Leningrad) in March 1918 Lenin and his wife, Nadezhda Krupskaya, lived for a week in a room in the hotel, No. 107. Uncharacteristically, this room has never become an object of veneration and is let to foreigners just like any other hotel room, although there is now talk of turning it into

31. National Hotel: A: looking up the central staircase. B: a private dining-room.

B

31C. National Hotel: one of the private dining-rooms prepared for deputies of the Supreme Soviet.

a special memorial. By the late 1920s the National resumed its function as a hotel for foreigners and among its notable guests were Anatole France and Paul Robeson.

Happily, the interior décor has not suffered brutal refurbishment over the years although the delightful pre-Revolutionary furniture – Art Nouveau lamps and heavy bronze statues – seems to be fast disappearing. Its restaurant and private dining-rooms are popular places in Moscow for wedding receptions and other special occasions. It is long overdue for a complete overhaul and will soon close its doors for a lengthy period. It is hoped that the result will not be to the detriment of its splendid public rooms.

· 32 ·

THE EXHIBITION OF ECONOMIC ACHIEVEMENTS

The Exhibition of Economic Achievements seems like a wry joke in today's Soviet Union, brutally aware of its economic backwardness compared to the West. But the Exhibition has had a long evolution during which the original concepts were turned on their heads.

It originated in 1923 as the All-Russia Agricultural Exhibition and opened in what is now Gorky Park. This first brave attempt to show the world that the Soviet Union could survive alone was also intended to educate the population in the processes of agriculture, and to raise the value of their labour in the eyes of the peasants. About fifty pavilions illustrating agricultural products were designed by the best architects, including Konstantin Melnikov, whose wooden Makhorka tobacco pavilion, based on the triangle and the cube, was the most daring. The exhibition closed after only three months.

A permanent agricultural exhibition complex began to be constructed in 1937 in another part of Moscow, the former park of the Sheremetiev estate at Ostankino. Unlike the humble, earlier exhibition, the achieve-

32. Exhibition of Economic Achievements: the entrance to the agricultural pavilion is on a Ukrainian theme.

ments of the Soviet state were to be empha-
sized and exaggerated in a patently obvious
propaganda exercise. Pavilions were to be
designed using the tenets of 'socialist realism', although confusion initially reigned
over what precisely this meant. For inst-
ance, the pavilion 'Ukraina' started life in
1937 as a wooden, many-sectored building.
In the same year it was entirely rebuilt so
that it resembled a richly decorated wall
with a large archway in the centre. In 1954
the same architect, Tatsy, again altered his
pavilion adding a belvedere with a crown
and spire, a common Soviet motif. Finally,
the pavilion was renamed 'Agriculture'.

In 1954 the exhibition, now adorned by
gigantic sculptures, was fundamentally re-
planned and expanded, with a grand
entranceway reminiscent of the Branden-
burg Gate. The layout had become strictly
symmetrical, the informal siting of the

early pavilions among the trees and lawns
of the park had given way to a line of
linked squares like a city street.

In 1959 the exhibition dropped the
appellation 'agricultural' and became the
Exhibition of Economic Achievements
(VDNKh) to promote the concept of Soviet
economic progress. With more pavilions,
ponds and fountains, it became something
of an amusement park for Sunday outings.
One of the most remarkable stands was an
Ilyushin airliner which small boys could
explore to their hearts' content. Other
exhibits include Atomic Energy, Cosmos
Education and Geology. More than 11
million visitors a year pour through the
gates of this monumental Potemkin village. Today, when the sober realities of the
Soviet economy have been fully revealed,
its exhibits look the worse for wear and the
whole concept seems outmoded.

· 33 ·

THE INSTITUTE OF ART HISTORY

This charming, modest house on two
floors flush with the street, is one of the few
remaining smaller houses that represents
both the early and mature periods of classical architecture in Moscow. Entry was,
as usual, from the courtyard and the principal rooms of the house were on the grand
first floor.

It was later acquired by the Lobkov
family who also owned a fine house on the
banks of the Moskva River opposite the
Kremlin. The mistress of the house, A.I.
Lobkova, supervised the construction in
1793-5, which entailed filling in the court-

33. Institute of Art History: an alcove in the ladies' marble drawing-room.

yard entrance and changing the doorway to the street side. Over the former courtyard entrance she added the most delightful room in the house, the oval-shaped drawing-room, which was either the ladies' withdrawing-room or divan-room. Its rich décor of light columns supporting the oval, painted ceiling, artificial marble walls and fine mouldings dates from the time of construction.

Madame Lobkova was the mother of one of Pushkin's closest friends, S.A. Sobolevsky, known as an ardent bibliophile. In 1828 Sobolevsky held a farewell party for the Polish poet, Adam Mickiewicz, during which Poland's national poet was presented with a silver goblet on which was inscribed the names of all his Moscow friends. Later, the house was purchased by the ubiquitous Golitsyn family. By the second half of the nineteenth century it had become an apartment house and in 1861 the great historian Klyuchevsky lived there as a university student.

At the end of the nineteenth century the pretty house was transformed into the City Printing House. After the Revolution and a period as apartments it was rescued by the Ministry of Culture, intelligently restored, and turned into the Institute of Art History, a much more congenial landlord. The Institute has been consistently more liberal and broader in its consideration of questions of art than the parallel Institute of the History of Fine Arts at the old Ivan Morozov House on Kropotkinskaya.

· 34 ·

OSTANKINO

Almost lost in the tall tower blocks that dominate the north of Moscow, standing incongruously next to the high television tower, is an elegant, delicately tinted house in classical style. This is the famous palace at Ostankino built by Count Nikolai Sheremetiev in the late eighteenth century in what was then the depths of the country as a theatre for his mistress, the actress Praskovia Zhemchugova.

The sumptuous palace owes its existence

A

B

34. Ostankino: A: the Blue Hall with artificial marble columns, painted ceiling and parquet floor. B: the Art Gallery with Dutch, Flemish, Italian and French paintings.

to the touching romance between the Count, one of the richest men in Russia, and the actress, who was one of his own serfs. The Count had the house/theatre built at Ostankino to enable Praskovia to perform in new surroundings and to escape the more stifling atmosphere of the old estate at Kuskovo. Praskovia and the Count, after years of living together, were married in 1800 to the displeasure of Moscow society, but the Countess enjoyed only three years of married life. She died in 1803 of tuberculosis just after the birth of her son, Dmitry. The Count did not survive her by very long and the little boy soon became an orphan and was looked after by guardians.

The grand house/theatre was built in the prevailing classical style by a group of well-known architects including the Russians Ivan Starov, Elizvoi Nazarov and Karl Blank, and the Italians working in Russia, Francesco Camporesi, Giacomo Quarenghi and Vincenzo Brenna. However, the overall supervision was arranged by the serf-architects Aleksei Mironov and Grigory Dikushin and later Pavel Argunov. The whole house with its magnificent theatre was finished in 1795 and Sheremctic gave the first of his famous elabo-

rate receptions, including a firework display, when the Polish Count Stanislas Potocki came to visit him.

The theatre, which forms the core of the main building, contained specially built-in machinery designed to move the stage and transform it into a ballroom in under an hour. The productions were mostly eighteenth-century operas, either Italian or Russian, with small casts. Recently the museum authorities at Ostankino have revived these operas, and in the warm Moscow summers one can enjoy the slightly stilted dramas and gentle music amid the august splendours of the theatre.

In 1797 an elaborate reception was staged for the coronation of Paul I, Catherine the Great's son who was assassinated only two years later. As the Emperor approached the drive to the palace, trees on both sides of the road, sawn through in advance, fell away to give a grand view of the palace. The Polish King, Stanislas Poniatowski, was likewise richly entertained only a week after Paul. The theatre fell into disuse after 1797 when the Count was ordered to St Petersburg to be with the moody new Emperor Paul, perceptively obsessed with the idea that he would be murdered.

34. *Ostankino: C: the Connecting Gallery joins the main palace to the Italian Pavilion. D: a detail of the ceiling.*

D

C

34E. Ostankino: the suite of drawing-rooms on the first floor.

34F. Ostankino: the Italian pavilion with antique sculpture.

However it was still used to receive Tsars during coronations in Moscow. In 1801 a splendid ball was staged during the coronation of Alexander I. During the Napoleonic invasion of 1812 the estate was occupied by French troops under Marshal Ney and during the retreat many of the theatre props and paintings were stolen. Nicholas I and his family paid a visit in 1851. In April 1856 Alexander II, the Tsar-Liberator, stayed for two weeks before his coronation. It is believed that discussions then took place between the Tsar and Count Dmitry Sheremetiev about the best ways of liberating the serfs. At any rate, Count Sheremetiev, as an experiment before the royal decree in 1861, gave his own serfs their freedom.

H

34. Ostankino. G: the theatre auditorium at the centre of the palace.
H: a view of the stage in the theatre.

By the end of the nineteenth century the grand house was seldom used, some of the living quarters separate from the main house were dismantled, and in 1913 it was leased to a foreign company. It was nationalized immediately after the Revolution and declared a museum in its own right and was therefore not maltreated under the Soviet regime – indeed it has been most carefully restored and cared for. It is one of the most beautiful surviving examples of the many mansions built in Moscow by the nobility at the end of the eighteenth century.

· 35 ·

THE METROPOLE HOTEL

The Metropole, almost adjacent to the Bolshoi Theatre on Theatre (Sverdlov) Square, is Moscow's largest pre-Revolutionary hotel and one in which the artistic fertility of the period received full expression.

Happily Savva Mamontov, a wealthy patron of the arts, was chief artistic adviser to the owners, the St Petersburg Insurance Society, and was well able to influence the choice of architects and artists to the great benefit of the building. Mamontov had established an artistic colony at his summer estate at Abramtsevo and was a close friend of the most outstanding artists of the day, many of whom were persuaded to participate in embellishing the Metropole.

Lev Kekushev, one of Moscow's leading Art Nouveau architects, was responsible for the overall design of the building and much of the initial interior décor. But the façade eventually chosen was to the design of William Walcot, a talented architect of the period. Walcot, born in Odessa of a Russian mother and English father, was to leave for England in 1906 shortly after the building of the hotel, his major architectural achievement. The focal points of the façade are the ceramic panels in rounded pediments, the major two, inspired by Edmond Rostand's popular play, *La Princesse Lointaine*, 'the Princess of Dreams', executed by Mikhail Vrubel.

The hotel's interior, originally decorated in Art Nouveau style, was partially redone in 1910 by Erikhson in classical style and this included the wonderful main dining-room lit by a huge glass canopy like a taut tent. Thus the rich interior is a curious mixture of the two opposing styles and each of the many public rooms is individually designed.

After the Revolution the Metropole became the Second House of the Soviets and meetings of the Central Executive Committee took place in the elegant dining-room attended by Lenin and Trotsky. Yakov Sverdlov, the first president of the USSR, had his office on the first floor and above, on the second, some offices of the Commissariat for Foreign Affairs were located. Yuri Chicherin, the first Commissar for Foreign Affairs, had a flat there as did Nikolai Bukharin, then editor of *Pravda*. By the late 1920s the building began to revert to use as a hotel. George Bernard Shaw stayed there when he visited Moscow in 1931 and had a two-hour meeting with Stalin.

In 1987 the hotel was closed for fundamental repairs and restoration work carried out by Finnish builders and Russian restorers. The Metropole, judged by some to be the most beautiful hotel in Europe, reopened in 1991.

35B. Metropole Hotel: an amusing ceiling in one of the small public rooms.

35C. Metropole Hotel: the stained-glass window faces both the staircase and the main dining-room.

35D. Metropole Hotel: the main dining-room with painted glazed roof.

THE SANDUNOVSKY STEAM BATHS

Steam baths are a vital part of Russian life. For centuries past they have been an inalienable part of even the meanest peasant's existence. A small wooden hut with a stove to heat the water drawn from river or lake stood on his property and provided the focus of his relaxation. Adam Olearius, the seventeenth-century German traveller, describes the shameful appearance of stark naked women cooling off from the baths on the streets of Moscow and accosting male passers-by; today's bathers are more modest. But even the introduction of modern bathrooms have made little dent on the popularity of Moscow's steam baths which are used annually by over 11 million people, or more than the total population.

There are some sixty-four steam baths in present-day Moscow, some relatively modern but many built in the nineteenth century. The two best-known baths are the Central and the Sandunovsky, both in the centre of the city. In 1806 Sila Sandunov, whose wife was a famous singer, built the first Sandunovsky baths, which were re-

36A. Sandunovsky Steam Baths: the ornate formal entrance with laundry.

built in 1895 in a mixture of moorish and baroque styles by B.V. Freydenberg. The main building on Neglinnaya with the marvellous archway and huge statues in niches on either side was for shops. Apartments or rooms to let were provided on the north side on Neglinnaya 2 Lane where Chekhov, who frequently used the baths, had a room. The baths proper, with men's and women's sections and luxuriously appointed private rooms, are set behind the main building along narrow lanes where sellers of birch twigs still accost customers. With their enormous chimneys, the baths occupy the steep hill, and take up nearly all the territory to the next street, Rozhdestvenka. Although the baths are becoming more and more dilapidated they can accommodate as many as 2,000 customers a day.

The baths are open six days a week, but Friday and Saturday evenings are the most popular times. Then clients can be seen clustered in the forecourt of the baths buying little bundles of birch twigs with their silvery leaves clinging. Within the confines of the steam room they happily flagellate themselves with the twigs to divest every pore of its accumulation of dirt. In the steam room steps lead up to benches where the hardened devotees gather and sweat it out, the most experienced recklessly throwing water on to the sizzling stove enveloping all in yet more scalding steam. The parboiled bather escapes to cool off in the pool, then enters the steam room again, and repeats the ritual until satisfied that he is well and truly purged. Russians are not embarrassed at their nakedness, although their heroic girths tend to surprise and flatter the occasional foreign bather. A wonderful relaxed feeling suffuses the entire body at the end of the bath. That is the time for indulgence in social gossip and the latest political news in comfortable cubicles drinking tea or, for the men, vodka. The bather can also take advantage of other services: he can visit the hairdresser, have his clothes repaired and pressed, or undergo a vigorous and stimulating massage. For many Muscovites the weekly ritual in the steam bath is something to look forward to, for the comradeship and news and the marvellous sense of physical ease.

36B. Sandunovsky Steam Baths: steam bath attendants ready to receive clients.

· 37 ·

THE HOUSE OF UNIONS
(THE NOBLES' CLUB)

Although dwarfed now by the 1930s Gosplan Building, the House of Unions, formerly the Nobles' Club, still gives an impression of discreet gentility in central Moscow. The building dates from 1780 when the new mansion of Prince Dolgoruky was completed by Matvei Kazakov, the exceptional classical architect. On the death of the Prince in 1784 Kazakov altered the mansion to prepare it for use as the Nobles' Club. The chief change which he effected was to enclose the courtyard and transform it with the use of twenty-eight Corinthian columns into the most elegant ballroom in Moscow. Following extensive alterations in 1908, it is only the Hall of Columns which survives from the original building.

The Nobles' Club is the most prominent mansion in Moscow and has witnessed many important historic events of the utmost variety. The Tsars often attended balls and concerts there when they were in the old capital. The last great ball before the Revolution was held in 1912 in celebration of the centenary of the Battle of Borodino against Napoleon.

A famous literary evening took place in the hall in June 1880, after the unveiling of the statue of Pushkin in Moscow when Dostoyevsky made his impassioned eulogy of Russia's national poet which provoked an extraordinary response. In his letter to his wife, Anna, Dostoyevsky wrote: 'When at the end I proclaimed the world-wide unity of mankind, the whole hall was in hysterics; when I finished – I cannot tell you the roars and yells of enthusiasm; people in the audience who were unknown to one another wept, sobbed, embraced each other and swore to be better men in the future . . .' The speech became a landmark in Russian literary history.

With the Soviet period the grand building entered the new era as the House of Unions. Although nominally under the trade unions' organization, it has harboured the most important state occasions since 1917. Among the many conferences and congresses the Eighth Congress of the Bolshevik Party in 1919 was unique, because Vladimir Tatlin's large model of his revolutionary communications and conference tower, never to be built, was displayed for all the delegates to admire.

In 1924 Lenin's body was displayed in the hall for five days of public mourning before being laid to rest in the wooden mausoleum hastily erected in the cruel January cold in Red Square. Since then the bodies of many political leaders have lain in the hall including that of Sergei Kirov, the murdered First Party Secretary of Leningrad, whose death Stalin instigated and then used as a pretext to begin his reign of terror. Stalin himself lay in state here on his death in March 1953. Ironically, the mourning was so intense that hundreds of people were crushed to death in the great crowds who came to pay homage to the cruel dictator.

The building has witnessed other gruesome spectacles: many of the show trials were staged there including the Metro-Vickers trial of several English engineers in 1933 and the trial in 1938 of Nikolai Bukharin, the communist theoretician who was called the darling of the Party by Lenin. The Chief Prosecutor who conducted this trial was the malevolent and perfidious Andrei Vyshinsky; Stalin was said to have watched the proceedings from the blackened window of a secret room high up in the hall.

But in the Soviet era the House of Unions has also maintained the more amiable nineteenth-century tradition of fine musical and literary occasions. Part of the Tchaikovsky music competition takes place in the grand hall and the anniversaries of great writers continue to be celebrated there. Political meetings are still held in the Hall of Columns, although they are more likely these days to be about ecology or the problems of education. On a lighter note, it is the traditional venue for the annual New Year's children's party visited by Grandfather Frost and his assistant, the Snow Maiden.

In 1990, in an astonishing turn-around, the Nobles' Club, after seventy years in the wilderness, is again holding its meetings in the old hall. Considering the mass emigration of the aristocracy following the Revolution and the persecution suffered by those who remained, it is surprising that so many have survived.

37. House of Unions: the Hall of Columns of the former Nobles' Club.

38. Moskva Restaurant: Soviet classicism prevails in the early 1930s dining-room.

THE MOSKVA RESTAURANT

In some ways the building of the Hotel Moskva epitomizes the grotesqueness of the Stalin era. Built in 1935-8, it was designed by Alexei Shchusev, the Vicar of Bray of Soviet architecture, who had proved readily adaptable to the variety of styles demanded by the new fashions of the era after the Revolution; he had built a workers' club and the Commissariat of Agriculture in the so-called constructivist style and had designed the coldly classical mausoleum that contains Lenin's body in Red Square. The success of the latter was to ensure for him the role of leading architect over the next two decades.

In 1924 the busy street of small shops and traders known as Hunters' Row was torn down in order to clear a site on this prime position in central Moscow. The intention was to erect a huge Palace of Labour. Sergei Kirov saw it thus: '. . . on that new, magnificent, splendid and revolutionary earth, we, the workers, born in miserable hovels, will leave those hovels in comradely ranks to enter our enchanted palaces . . .' Many novel and innovative designs were submitted in the competition for the palace, including the Vesnin brothers' highly original constructivist proposal. But disagreements arose over the results of the competition and it was never built. By the 1930s, as Stalin consolidated

his power the political climate had altered and with it architectural fashion. It was decided to build a hotel on the cleared site.

From the wide space in front of the Manege next to the entrance to Red Square, the Hotel Moskva looks sombre and forbidding. Its heavy design fails to justify its domineering position on the huge, asphalt square. However, a second look confirms what might have been missed at first glance; the façade is entirely asymmetrical. The right and left wings are executed quite differently; the left more elaborate, with pilasters and high arched windows, while decoration on the right is confined to the balconies. The explanation for this apparent extraordinary lapse on the part of the chief architect of the Soviet neo-classical period might seem bizarre, but considering the atmosphere generated by the absolute and arbitrary rule of Stalin, quite believable. Shchusev presented two versions of the same plan to Stalin for his approval intending him to choose the variant he preferred. Stalin assumed it was a single design and approved the whole plan as it stood. No one dared go back to him to explain the error and so it was built, lop-sided.

It is a pleasing irony that the Moskva, whose façade bears such a vivid reminder of Stalin's arbitrary rule, is now used to accommodate the deputies of the new democratically elected Supreme Soviet. Members of the public can be seen lobbying the deputies on their way to and from sessions of the Soviet parliament.

39

THE KOMSOMOL THEATRE
(THE MERCHANTS' CLUB)

In 1909 the handsome Merchants' Club on Malaya Dmitrova (Chekhov Street) was completed by Illarion Ivanov-Shits, a major architect of the early years of the century. The merchants had for some years been crowded in unprepossessing accommodation further down the same road and were anxious to have specially constructed premises. The merchants − business men, factory owners, bankers − were a clearly defined class in pre-Revolutionary Moscow, inferior in the social scale to the nobility, but by 1900 the giants of Russia's industrial revolution.

Many of the merchants, therefore, became very rich in a very short time. Although often depicted as lacking culture and rapaciously greedy for money, many, like the Morozovs and Soldatenkovs, used their wealth to endow hospitals and poor houses and build inexpensive apartment blocks. It is strange that the merchants, brought up in the conservative atmosphere of the Old Believers, were attracted by contemporary art and became the chief patrons of Art Nouveau.

Their own club was in the Art Nouveau style, which is particularly evident through the rich, linear interiors, although Ivanov-Shits preferred a mock classical exterior.

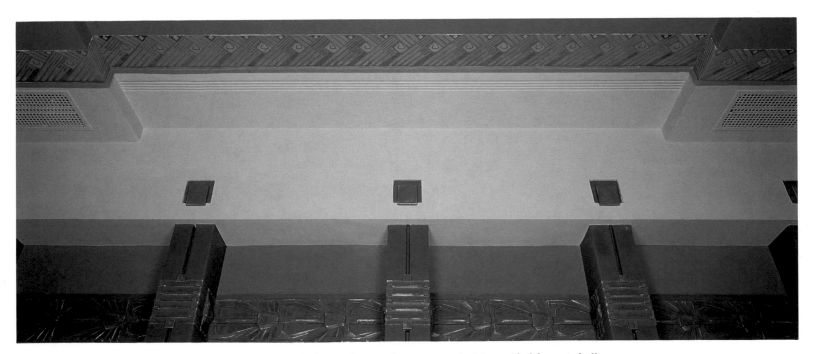

39A. Komsomol Theatre: lines and squares are the leit motif of the main hall.

Inside it is sumptuously attired with expensive woods, stone and entrances like Egyptian tombs. The unfortunate merchants, however, enjoyed their club for only a few years, for it was closed and peremptorily confiscated after the Revolution.

In January 1918, just before the Soviet government moved to Moscow, anarchists (who had supported the Bolsheviks before the Revolution) occupied the building turning everything topsy-turvy. It was not until April that the Cheka, the forerunners of the KGB, were able to surround and take the building by force and expel the anarchists.

After a period as a Party school and a cinema, it became in 1933 the interesting Theatre of Working Youth (TRAM) which

was closed three years later when the massive reorganization of all the arts occurred. It reopened as the Theatre of the Lenin Komsomol which did not have a particularly distinguished history for many years, but in the mid-80s was in the forefront of *glasnost* with a daring production of Shatrov's *Dictatorship of Conscience* which discussed the pros and cons of Soviet socialism with participation from the audience. It was the first Moscow theatre to stage rock operas and after a four-year battle with the censors, an experimental play by a woman author, Petrushevskaya, *Three Girls in Blue*, was performed which explored with Chekhovian echoes the hardships and loneliness of Soviet women.

39B. Komsomol Theatre: doorways leading to the offices of the former Merchants' Club.

· 40 ·

DANIEL MITLYANSKY, THE SCULPTOR

Daniel Mitlyansky is a sculptor working in wood and plaster who has his studio in the north of Moscow. Born in 1924, his career spans the repressive late Stalin period through the vicissitudes of the Khrushchev era and the stifling lassitude of Brezhnev to the growing candour under Gorbachev. He is most at home making naïve figures on historical and political themes, subjects which he can now openly tackle. His work in the series with historical titles like 'Europe and Russia' or 'We Need Perestroika' is a direct response to the changes going on in the USSR today. Like many artists he is reaping unexpected benefits with offers of trips abroad and exhibitions at home. His stature is such that he was invited to make the death mask of Andrei Sakharov, the famous scientist and public figure, who died in December 1989.

Sculpture in the Soviet Union has traditionally had a major political role to play. Even before the Revolution there was a penchant for public statuary extolling the virtue and victories of generals or Tsars. However, the experimental verve and sheer outpouring of talent in the world of painting in the period just before and after the Revolution was not reflected in Russian sculpture. Sculptors remained realists steeped in the academic teaching of the art schools, their work dull and uninspired. In designing the busts for Lenin's Plan of Monumental Propaganda in 1918, revolutionary content was not matched by revolutionary form; the few talented sculptures like the cubist bust of Bakunin were violently attacked in the press. Bakunin was left covered for a long time; when the bust was finally exposed after the boards protecting it had been stolen for firewood, it was promptly demolished.

Vladimir Tatlin did design a monument to the Revolution that befitted the idea of the new society and was like sculpture on a grand scale. In 1920 he completed a model of the famous Tatlin Tower, the monument to the Third International, of glass cylinder, cone and cube, all three structures to revolve at different times. This constructivist masterpiece was never built and the avant-garde movement in painting

40. *Daniel Mitlyansky: the sculptor's studio with wooden and plaster figures.*

41A. St Pimen: the modern iconostasis by Fyodor Shekhtel was executed about 1900.

unusual white marble icon screen designed by Fyodor Shekhtel.

St Pimen's was to play a singular role in Church history after the Revolution. The newly elected Patriarch, Tikhon, at first fought against the demands of the Soviet regime, particularly after the murder of the Tsar and his family. At the same time a pro-Soviet movement against the Patriarch was fostered among the lesser or 'white' (married) clergy, advocating reforms such as replacing Old Slavonic with Russian. St Pimen's became the centre of this 'Living' or 'Red' Church under Archpriest Alexander Vvedensy, a leader and great orator.

In 1922 Patriarch Tikhon was arrested and after nearly a year in prison published a statement in which he promised to cease opposing the Soviet regime. This effectively undermined the position of the Living Church which nevertheless continued to exist until the 1940s. The Patriarch died in 1925 and his successor, Metropolitan Sergius, whose views were also tempered by a spell in prison, published the famous statement in which he identified the Orthodox Church completely with the trials and tribulations of the Soviet Union.

In spite of this act of submission the Church suffered dreadfully in the fanatical anti-religious movement of the 1930s. In 1935 the Holy Synod, the central governing organ of the Church, was disbanded and at the height of the terror – 1937 and 1938 – priests (including those of the Living Church) were a natural target and suffered executions and arrest on a huge scale. Even the arrest of Metropolitan Sergius was contemplated. Nearly all church buildings in the Soviet Union were at that time closed; in Moscow only about five were left functioning, including St Pimen's.

The Church was saved by the outbreak of war in 1941. The Soviet authorities quickly realized that assistance from the Church was vital in the revival of patriotic feeling to defeat the aggressor, and a *modus vivendi* was agreed when Stalin received the three most senior Metropolitans in 1943. Elections were allowed to enable Sergius to be declared Patriarch. With this development the Living Church completely disintegrated, its priests submitting to the new Patriarch; those who had acquired superior rank relinquished it and returned to their previous station. Thus St Pimen's returned to the traditional Orthodox Church.

and architecture, to which the monument belonged, declined by the end of the 1920s with the rise of Stalin.

The demand for statuary by the regime, especially busts of Lenin, appeared to be insatiable. It meant that artists like Mitlyansky could earn a good wage on commissions for Lenin busts and at the same time pursue his own artistic inclinations within the limits imposed by the current official policy towards the arts. His studio is located in an impressive modern studio block for artists that was meant to have been opened for the Youth Festival in 1957 as a showcase illustrating how well artists live in the USSR. Unfortunately, it was only completed two years after the festival.

· 41 ·

THE CHURCH OF ST PIMEN THE GREAT

The picturesque St Pimen the Great in the New Gatekeepers' (Novyye Vorotniki) settlement provides a splendid touch of colour in the drabness of the proliferating tower blocks surrounding it. Built in 1658 with later additions, it is situated just outside the Garden Ring Road, the former boundary of Moscow. In the early years of this century the interior was repainted and the traditional iconostasis replaced by the

41B. St Pimen: a view from the side chapel.

42. Bolshoi Theatre: a view of the tiers and royal box from the stage.

· 42 ·

THE BOLSHOI THEATRE

After the Kremlin and St Basil's, the Bolshoi (Large) Theatre with its familiar façade of columns, pediment and sculpture of Apollo driving the flying chariot, is possibly the best-known building in Moscow.

Surprisingly, the founding of the Bolshoi is partly due to the efforts of a remarkable Englishman, Michael Maddox. In 1780 Maddox built a large theatre, the Petrov, on the banks of the Neglinnaya River where the Bolshoi is now situated. The Petrov Theatre could accommodate 1,000 theatre-goers, was lit by forty-two crystal chandeliers and had a special round hall with mirrors for masquerades and balls. It functioned for twenty-five years, but then, in 1805, caught fire and was utterly destroyed in a single day. Maddox, who had been declared bankrupt in 1789 but had remained as director of the Imperial Theatre (as it was then known), never recovered from this blow and died in the provinces in poverty. It was not until twenty years later, in 1824, after the Napoleonic invasion that a new theatre, designed by Professor Mikhailov from St Petersburg under the supervision of city architect Osip Bove, was constructed and completed.

In 1853 the theatre again suffered a disastrous fire which began at the back of the stage on which some seventy children, orphans from the Foundling Home, were rehearsing. Fortunately the children were saved, but the fire burned for two days and destroyed the theatre. It was restored and largely rebuilt by Albert Cavos, the architect of the Mariinsky Theatre in St Petersburg and an authority on acoustics. Cavos enlarged the theatre to a capacity of over 2,000 seats making it one of the most splendid in Europe with a stage much larger than La Scala or the Paris Opéra. He added another floor which, with its pediment, provides the rather awkward backdrop to the sculpture of Apollo and his racing chariot. Its reopening in 1856 coincided with the coronation of Alexander II and the Tsar graciously attended the ceremony.

At first the Bolshoi Company was considered inferior to the Mariinsky in St Petersburg – indeed, for some years it was obliged to share the theatre with an Italian company. However, by the end of the century its golden age arrived when Tchaikovsky's *Swan Lake* had its première. Rachmaninov conducted, Chaliapin sang and stage sets were designed by artists of the calibre of Vasnetsov and Korovin.

After the Bolshevik Revolution in 1917 the fate of the theatre was for a time in doubt, but Lunacharsky, the energetic Commissar for Enlightenment, led the battle to restore opera and ballet and by the mid-1920s the Bolshoi was putting on new productions like the ballet *The Red Poppy* by Glier and Prokofiev's *Love of Three Oranges*. Since then it has gone from strength to strength with music by Shostakovich and Khachaturyan and stars such as Ulanova and Plisetskaya.

The Bolshoi is also used for government and Party meetings. Perhaps the most dramatic was in July 1918, when, after the 5th All-Russian Congress of the Soviets the left-socialist revolutionaries attempted a coup. Their leader, Mariya Spiridonova, and her colleagues remained prisoners in the theatre until the coup was put down. The Bolshoi is still used occasionally for Party and State occasions, but the most important events now take place in the Kremlin Palace of Congresses. The royal box, formerly the Tsar's box, is now only used for important State leaders and foreign visitors.

43A. Peter Palace: a detail of the plasterwork.

· 43 ·

THE PETER PALACE
(ZHUKOV AIR ACADEMY)

The route into Moscow from Sheremetiev International Airport along Leningrad Prospekt is lined by a procession of sombre neo-classical buidings suddenly interrupted by a riotous red and white Gothic/neo-Russian palace set behind curving crenellated walls of matching design. This is the Peter Travel Palace (Petrovsky Putevoi Dvorets) built in the eighteenth century (1775-82) by Matvei Kazakov, the leading classical architect. The palace, located on the St Petersburg highway, was to provide a place to rest and change after the arduous journey of 400 miles by carriage to Moscow.

All coronations in the old Kremlin required the presence of the new Emperor or Empress for several weeks at the beginning of each reign. Nicholas II with Alexandra was the last monarch to use the Peter Palace during his coronation in 1896. And it was from there that the new Tsar and Tsarina were to witness a tragic event, the ominous start to an ill-fated reign. The Peter Palace was conveniently located across the road from the Khodynka Field where, on the day after the coronation so many people crowded into the field for the traditional distribution of gifts that, when the beer wagons were brought up, a stampede ensued and over a thousand people, mostly women and children, were trampled to death. From the balcony of the Peter Palace Nicholas and Alexandra watched the dead being carted away. There they were prevailed upon by Nicholas's domineering uncles to attend the French ambassador's ball that evening. To the great dismay and disgust of the general population, they did so and even danced.

Another prominent guest at the palace, albeit an uninvited one, was Napoleon Bonaparte. In September 1812 he marched into Moscow at the head of his vast army, encountering a city virtually bereft of its population, and almost immediately the great conflagration began. Napoleon, who was residing in the Kremlin, was forced to flee in the middle of the night with his entourage to the relative safety of the Peter Palace whence he watched the copper flames of the burning city in the distance.

43B. Peter Palace: looking up into the painted dome of the circular hall.

Although Napoleon remained in Moscow only thirty-three days, he managed to inflict considerable damage on the palace which was only made good in 1840.

The palace is laid out in red brick with white-stone trim rather in the fashion of the Moscow baroque of a century earlier, although here the large flat dome and the interior are purely classical. It exhibits an unusual blend of Gothic, medieval Russian and classical motifs intermingled to form a harmonious, balanced but vigorous building unique in Moscow. The park behind and to the south was laid in 1827 by Adam Menelaws, the English architect, who was so active in St Petersburg.

After the Revolution, in 1923, the palace became the home of the prestigious Zhukov Air Academy who keep the principal grand rooms in a fine state of repair.

· 44 ·

THE SAVOY RESTAURANT

The Savoy Hotel, built in 1912 in response to the growing need in Moscow for central, first-class hotels, was designed by V.A. Velichkin for the well-known insurance company, 'Salamander', the emblem of which, a small salamander, can still be seen on the walls. It is interesting that of Moscow's major pre-Revolutionary hotels, three — the National, Metropole and Savoy — were built between 1901 and 1912 and that they are all still in use.

The Savoy, its name surely borrowed from the prestigious London hotel, ranks third after the National and the Metropole. After the Revolution it was nationalized and turned into a hostel for members of the Commissariat for Foreign Affairs whose offices were in a huge apartment block on nearby B. Lubyanka (Dzerzhinsky) Street; housing was such a problem that the new commissariats had to find accommodation for their own employees. By the beginning of the 1930s the Savoy had again reverted to a hotel. Among its guests was Henri Barbusse, the French socialist, who wrote a sycophantic biography of Stalin.

In 1958 the name of the hotel was changed to the Berlin to emphasize Moscow's good relations with East Germany and the restaurant began to specialize in German cooking. It continued to be

44. *Savoy Restaurant: the fountain is reflected in the ceiling mirrors.*

one of Moscow's better-class hotels, if rather shabby, until, in 1987, it entered a new phase. The first of the Moscow hotels to conclude an agreement with a foreign firm, it became jointly managed by the Soviet tourist organization, Intourist, and the Finnish air company, Finnair. Their plan to transform the old hotel into one of luxury class has been realized with the aid of a Yugoslav construction firm. There is air conditioning in every room, modern bathrooms and even alarm clocks. If in the past foreigners travelling individually had a hard time finding accommodation in Moscow, nowadays it is the turn of tourist groups to suffer in this way as the battle for hard currency is waged by the hotels.

Tourist groups are not admitted to the likes of the Savoy (its old name returned when it opened in 1989) which charges businessmen up to $500 a night. But the quality of the service, provided by Russian staff with a leavening of Finns, is unrivalled elsewhere in Moscow.

The Savoy restaurant, always one of the most attractive in Moscow, is now fully restored to its former, heavily ornate, glory. The almost rococo effect of the fountain and swirling gold plasterwork of the ceiling with its reflecting mirrors is quite overwhelming. Combined with a good chef and efficient service it has become one of Moscow's best places to eat in — if you can afford it.

· 45 ·

MAX BIRSTEIN, THE ARTIST

The puckish figure of the artist, Max Birstein, now in his eighth decade, accurately reflects his cheerful outlook on life. A skilled artist of portraits and still lifes, he declares he owes his inspiration to Marc Chagall and to the cubist artist of landscapes, Robert Falk, the great teacher of Birstein's generation.

Although his teachers were pre-Revolutionary artists, Birstein is a product of Soviet art education. He was able to exhibit almost immediately on graduation from the Surikov Art Institute in 1939; his work even received the highest accolade, praise in *Pravda*. In 1943 he became a member of the all-important Union of Artists which enabled him to travel abroad as well as enjoy the usual benefits of commissions, dacha and studio. In the 1950s and 60s he made many journeys to the Middle East and Africa and his work was purchased by the Tretyakov Gallery. In 1968 his work was exhibited in France, Japan and Sweden as part of an exhibition of official Soviet art. His first visit to London was on a personal invitation in 1989. It made a strong impression on him and he began painting London street scenes; a view of Tower Bridge can be seen in the background of the photograph.

Birstein has a huge and amusing collection of figures of cats of all sizes and makes, which he adds to whenever the opportunity presents itself. Surprisingly, he prefers dogs as pets. The chair on which his feet rest was carved by the artist Sergei Malyutin, a follower of the arts and crafts neo-Russian tradition, who designed the fantastic Pertsov apartment house in Moscow, its façade embellished with ancient Russian motifs. It was in this house that Robert Falk had his studio and the chair, one of six purchased from the descendants of Malyutin, has a special significance for the artist. It was made at the famous arts and crafts artists' colony supported by Princess Tenisheva at Talashkino.

According to Birstein the following system was employed to ensure one's work was accepted by the Union of Artists.

45. Max Birstein: the artist in his studio, his feet resting on a Malyutin chair.

Three paintings would be presented to the Commission; they invariably chose the one which in the eyes of the artist was the worst. Next time round the artist presented only his poorest paintings. That, says Max, is how the union educated its members.

· 46 ·

THE CONFECTIONERY SHOP 'ARMENIA'

In the corner of a gloomy building which faces both Tverskaya (Gorky) Street at Pushkin Square and the Boulevard is the confectionery shop, 'Armenia'. It is a popular shop where special Armenian delicacies can sometimes be found like delicious walnut jam. The lavish interior is more than a little surprising. Here, not only the carefully executed ceilings with colourfully painted medallions circling the Art Deco-style light fittings, the mouldings and interesting floor tiling, but the furniture itself, mahogany cupboards with brass fittings and pediments, seem to stem from the period of fine craftsmanship at the beginning of the century. Yet it is not a shop built about 1900 designed for a rich merchant seeking to impress the public, like Yeliseyev's Food Hall across the road, but a product of the Soviet era, completed in 1940.

It is situated in block 'G' of the buildings erected in 1935-40 on the reconstructed Tverskaya (Gorky) Street. Moscow's narrow and winding main thoroughfare was considered inappropriate by the Bolshevik

46. Confectionery 'Armenia': the elaborate interior was completed in 1940.

leadership for the capital of the world's first socialist state. Drastic plans were made to straighten it and make it three times wider. This involved not only demolition and new construction, but physically moving some buildings back into the old courtyards like the splendid Savvinskoe Podvore (in the courtyard of No. 6) and the old building of the Governor-General of Moscow, now the City Council. In the process of reconstruction, one monastery and several churches were demolished including one that stood on the site of the 'Armenia', the Church of Dmitry Solunsky, built in 1791, an interesting example of early classicism.

The massive seven-storey block occupied by the 'Armenia' with shops on the ground floor and fine, large apartments above, was designed by Arkady Mordvinov, the architect of most of the new monumental buildings on Gorky Street. A Party member at the age of twenty-five, he had dabbled in constructivist architecture before becoming, by the mid-1930s, one of the most ardent adherents of the decorative style of Soviet neoclassicism. He is also credited with the introduction of pre-fabricated housing.

· 47 ·

METRO BELORUSSKAYA

Belorusskaya Metro Station connects the radial Gorkovsko-Zamoskvoretskaya Line and the Circle Line with the Belorussian Railway Station (formerly the Brest), which serves Poland, the Baltic States and western Europe via Belorussia.

The Circle Line which began construction in 1944 before the end of the war set out to link the already existing radial lines in a great arc. It repeats underground the traditional street system of Moscow with its radial, concentric roads. The underground Circle Line lies a little beyond the surface Garden Ring Road and connects seven of the nine railway stations of Moscow. It was a necessary development in the metro system to relieve the centre of heavy traffic. The line descends deep into the ground, constructed in some places, including Belorusskaya, under the existing earlier station. Because the stations are set so deep the escalators, fast as they are, take a long time to reach the platforms, and

47. *Metro Belorusskaya: the arched hall converges on the figures holding the coat of arms of Belorussia.*

transfers are a lengthy business. The commission for the interior design of the halls was for monumental forms, sculptures and mosaic murals on the theme of the 'military glory' of the Soviet people in the war and their 'peaceful, creative toil'. Projects were submitted to closed competitions in which groups of architects rather than individuals took part.

The Belorusskaya Station on the Circle Line opened in 1952. Its hall is particularly splendid, escaping the ostentatious, even vulgar, extremes of some of the other stations on this line although the theme, 'the peaceful labour of the Belorussian people' seems a little banal. White and beige-coloured marble distinguishes the walls; on the plaster ceiling are rhythmically placed hexagonal mosaic panels by G. Opryshko of flower-bedecked Belorussians in national costume engaged in day-to-day activities. The tessellated floor, a traditional Belorussian pattern like a rich carpet, is especially effective. Three figures at the back support the coat of arms of Soviet Belorussia on which is emblazoned, 'proletarians of all countries, unite!'. Another sculptural group of Belorussian partisans is placed in the transit hall; Belorussia was in the front line when the Germans invaded and was not liberated until 1944. Its extensive forests made it ideal terrain for partisan warfare.

· 48 ·

METRO MAYAKOVSKAYA

Moscow's earliest metro stations were opened in 1935; the station Mayakovskaya was part of the second phase, the Gorkovsko-Zamoskvoretskaya Line, which was completed in 1938. It was designed by Aleksei Dushkin, a distinguished Soviet architect of several of the early metro stations as well as the children's department store, 'Children's World'. It was called after the famous poet of the Revolution, Vladimir Mayakovsky, the writer of satirical and political poetry and plays eulogizing the Revolution and attacking its bourgeois opponents. Mayakovsky had joined the Bolshevik Party as early as 1908 and, although originally associated with the futurists, quickly developed his own unique, rhetorical style using the language and images of the street. This unre-

fined propaganda poetry of everyday speech with its complex rhyming pattern dovetailed with the political aspirations of the early days of the Revolution. However, by the mid-1920s his individual approach began to conflict with that of the authorities and his two satirical plays, *The Bedbug* and *The Bathhouse*, were coolly received by officialdom. In 1930, these disappointments and personal problems led to Mayakovsky committing suicide. Stalin, initially hostile to Mayakovsky, declared in 1935 that his work was the model for Socialist Realism and in the same year the important square at the junction of Tverskaya (Gorky) Street and the Garden Ring was renamed in his honour.

The palatial early metro stations are the most beautiful and the hall of Mayakovskaya, in succeeding arches of light and dark marble, is generally regarded as the best of them. The grey and black marble is offset by polished stainless steel columns that support the roof, an interesting combination of steel and stone. The thirty-six oval cupolas providing the lighting coincide with the arches; high up in the domes, mosaic smalt (cobalt blue glass) panels add a touch of colour to the sombre columns. The mosaics were designed in 1938-9 by A.A. Deineka, a prosaic artist of the Revolution who became popular in the Stalin period. A model of the station won the Grand Prix at the World Fair in New York in 1938.

Mayakovskaya Station is famous not only for its splendid design, but for the historic role it played on 6 November 1941. The early metro lines were laid deep underground so that they could be converted to bomb shelters should war break out. In November 1941 German troops were rapidly closing in on Moscow and bombs were falling on the partially evacuated city. Because of its deep and spacious hall, Mayakovskaya was chosen as the venue of the traditional celebration on the eve of the 24th anniversary of the Revolution. The entire politburo and invited guests filled the station hall. Stalin calmly described the military situation, admitting that Russian troops had several times fewer tanks than the Germans. Next day, the usual military parade was held in Red Square where Stalin made an impassioned speech invoking for the first time the examples of the saints and warriors of old Russia.

48. Metro Mayakovskaya: the most successful of the early metro stations.

METRO CHEKHOVSKAYA

The underground system in Moscow is continually expanding ever further from the old centre. In 1987 a new line, the Serpukhovskaya, was opened running north-south through the centre and reaching the outlying areas of Moscow hitherto poorly served by fast transport.

Chekhovskaya is one of the new stations on this line and is located under Pushkin Square and connected there with two other metro stations on two other lines, Pushkinskaya (1975) and Gorkovskaya (1979) [now renamed Tverskaya]. Thus three major Russian writers are celebrated in three halls of the underground system under the famous statue of Pushkin. Gorkovskaya was named after Maxim Gorky, who opposed the Revolution, but later became an apologist for the Soviet regime and official founder of socialist realism. Pushkinskaya is named after Alexander Pushkin, the founder of literary Russian and the greatest poet of the Russian language, and Chekhovskaya after Anton Chekhov, the unsurpassed short-story writer and dramatist of the turn of the century. Gorky had no connection with this part of Moscow other than the fact that Gorky Street (now again named Tverskaya) which borders Pushkin Square, was named after him. Pushkin's association comes from his famous statue erected in 1880 which, for the first seventy years of its existence, stood across Tverskaya (Gorky) Street on the Boulevard and was only moved to its present site in 1949. Nevertheless, the Russians' feeling for their finest poet is such that every 6 June on the anniversary of his birth, thousands of people gather before the statue to recite his poetry which everyone knows by heart.

The peripatetic Chekhov had a closer association with the area; on a nearby

49. Metro Chekhovskaya: A: the solitary artist evokes the disillusion implicit in Chekhov's characters. B: flowers representing love and beauty are a tribute to the author. C: the dead bird with outstretched wings identifies The Seagull. *D: the comfortable interior with guitar is a typical Chekhov stage setting. E: the writer often described similar provincial towns. F: the elegant woman at the gazebo suggests the longing expressed in* Lady with a Dog.

A

D

B

C

E

F

street named after him he lived at four different addresses at various times in his life. The metro station in his name has been charmingly decorated with pretty marble mosaics by Lyudmilla and Pyotr Shorchev which evoke the atmosphere here of his stories and plays like *Lady with a Dog* and *The Cherry Orchard*. It is interesting that although new stations further down the line in the outskirts are not being especially decorated, it has been decided that the new ones in the centre such as Chekhovskaya should be designed in an interesting and attractive manner in line with the older stations.

· 50 ·

VERA, VALERY AND THE CHUIKOVS

Russian hospitality is legendary and no more so in this huge bustling city than in the apartment of Vera and Valery Nanivskaya-Ivanov. They live on the northern edge of Moscow near the River Station in a fourteen-storey block of flats for artists erected in 1974. Although they are not artists themselves, they have by this accident of accommodation become closely involved in the artists' colony of their block, sharing their problems during difficult times and enjoying their successes now that most barriers to exhibitions and travel abroad have been lifted.

Vera began her career as a teacher of English at the psychology faculty of the University of Moscow but has, since learning Japanese, broadened her research to include moral education in Japan; she now also teaches a course on oriental religion. Recently, she has changed course from this academic line to dabbling in the world of art exhibitions; her industry and good eye

50. *Vera and Valery (foreground) entertain the Chuikov family.*

51A. Olympic Complex: the training rink.

led to an exhibition of selected artists in Cambridge in November 1990 and London in 1991. Valery not only supports her in this venture but has two careers of his own as a cameraman for Mosfilm and as a fine tailor of clothes for women, a valuable sideline in Moscow starved for fashion.

Their friends, the artist Ivan Chuikov, his wife, Galina, a ceramist and their daughter, Yevgeniya, an art student, are neighbours. Ivan is one of the leading Soviet modern artists, formerly a 'conceptualist' although he now describes his work as post-modern, who is enjoying deserved success in Germany and England. For most of his career in Moscow his paintings were not exhibited; even today, the state galleries in the Soviet Union have yet to purchase his work. His highly original paintings are distinguished by the use of strong lines and colours depicting sharply angled windows or doors or paintings directly on glass.

The warm, inviting apartment consists, as is usual in Moscow, of only two rooms plus kitchen and bathroom; books and paintings compete for the limited space. In the background are paintings by contemporary artists including one by Ivan Chuikov (upper right). On the table is the enticing feast which Vera, Ukrainian by nationality and a most accomplished cook, conjures up apparently effortlessly at the appearance of even the most unexpected guests.

······························

· 51 ·

······························

THE OLYMPIC COMPLEX

······························

The huge Olympic complex, including stadium and swimming-pool, was built in 1975-80 next to Moscow's only functioning mosque just north of the Garden Ring Road for the Olympic Games of 1980. Although the withdrawal of many countries, including the USA, from participation after the Soviet invasion of Afghanistan diminished the success of the games, Moscow did profit by gaining several large new sports complexes. The group of buildings on what is now Olympiisky Prospekt is among the most spectacular.

The principal architect was once again Mikhail Posokhin, Chief Architect of Moscow from 1960-83, and responsible more than anyone else for the imposition of the international modern style in those years. Here with his team of architects and engineers, he created some striking buildings which unfortunately he chose to cover in concrete, a material which does not weather well in Moscow. The huge enclosed stadium with seating for a maximum of 45,000 is in the form of an ellipse covered with a thin membrane; it is entirely lit from within by artificial light. A great gold-coloured aluminium band encircles the stadium like a crown suggesting the Olympic torch.

The stadium central arena has been so constructed that it can be moved and transformed to fulfil various functions. As a football stadium — a sport as popular in the USSR and as passionately followed as in Europe — it can seat 35,000. But it can also be adjusted by moving the walls to make it suitable for light athletics, heavy athletics, a circus, theatrical performances, youth dances, New Year parties, or film festivals. This very versatile building was also used at Easter in April 1990, to stage a huge religious pop concert in which Alla Pugacheva, the popular singer, took part — an event scarcely foreseen in the original concept of the constructors.

The stadium can also be transformed, at any time of year, into an ice-rink where ice-hockey games take place, the second most favourite sport after football. A training rink for skating enthusiasts is situated to one side of the main stadium. Skating is a hugely popular sport which, in a normally cold winter, is enjoyed by nearly every child and many adults in the many open rinks, iced-over ponds, and on the flooded paths of the great expanse of Gorky Park. The careers of Soviet international skating stars are followed with as much interest as those of pop stars. A well-appointed gymnastics arena is also provided in the complex for training in a sport in which the Soviet Union has achieved international pre-eminence.

The splendid Olympic swimming-pool, which is located in a smaller building next

51B. Olympic Complex: working out in the gym.

to the stadium, can also be divided into sections for swimming and diving competitions. Members of the Moscow public can use the swimming-pool at certain times.

· 52 ·

THE CHURCH OF THE TIKHVIN VIRGIN

From the fourteenth century it became the custom (and still is) to make pilgrimages to the most holy Monastery of the Trinity/St Sergius some fifty miles north of Moscow at what is now Zagorsk. Among the pil-

grims were the Tsars themselves who would relieve the long walk with frequent pauses for rest and food, often seizing the opportunity of taking their falcons into the countryside to hunt in the forests.

In time the route became lined with 'travel palaces', large wooden houses where the Tsar and his considerable entourage could spend the night or several days on their way to the monastery. One such travel palace was at the first stop, a village now well within contemporary Moscow known as Alekseyevskoye after Tsar Aleksei Mihailovich, father of Peter the Great. Aleksei, the 'angelic' Tsar who was known for his saintliness, made his first pilgrimage at the age of four months and thereafter

would set out for the monastery once a year. Preparations, which were vast, involved the supply of feed for hundreds of horses, falcons for hunting, and a huge baggage train.

The wooden travel palace no longer exists, but the tall elegant brick church built in 1676-80 which was connected to the palace — the old door can be seen on the north side — is still standing and open for services. The Church of the Tikhvin Virgin, named after a revered icon, is situated high on what used to be the banks of a stream surrounded by an old graveyard. In winter its unusual blue cupolas and red walls with white detailing are visible from a long way off. Inside the beautiful iconostasis, like

52. Tikhvin Virgin Church: the eighteenth-century iconostasis.

the frescoes, was fashioned in the eighteenth century. One can imagine the Tsars and their boyars at prayer here after a successful hunt in the surrounding woods with their falcons.

· 53 ·

LYUDMILA OSMUSHINA, THE FASHION DESIGNER

Lyudmila Osmushina is one of a new breed of Muscovites. Now in her thirties, she made her career as a fashion designer before *glasnost*, but it is only in recent years that she has been able to realize her potential. One of many unknown Moscow fashion designers who have begun to make their name, she is distinguished by her striking originality. With her husband, Vladimir, she runs a boutique in the sports buildings constructed for the 1980 Olympics not far from the centre of Moscow and the old House of Models.

Here she hangs her startling clothes from the ceiling to display them to full advantage. The black and white dresses represent for her a particular philosophy; the black is evil struggling against the pure white of the soul. She also likes to use fur in the clothes she designs; in dresses as well as outdoor clothing. Although it has become unpopular and unfashionable in the West to use fur, the Russian winter makes its use seem entirely reasonable. One of her central interests is in improving the technology of the rag trade to make mass production of clothing more efficient and faster to react to changes in fashion.

Russians have long been accustomed to making their own clothes and are extremely fashion conscious; there was a time when one of the best gifts a Westerner could bring his Russian friends was a copy of *Vogue*. Indeed, clothes consciousness is so great that Russians frequently cannot understand the attitude of many Westerners who, although they could obviously afford to dress well, prefer to appear in torn jeans, T-shirts and sneakers.

Lyudmila has exhibited abroad and will be part of the exhibition 'Out of Russia' in London in 1991.

53. Lyudmila Osmushina fashions hang from the ceiling.

54A. *Tolstoy House: the dining-room set for dinner looks on to the garden.*

WEST MOSCOW

The districts west of the Kremlin were settled in the eighteenth and nineteenth centuries by the upper classes and, in this century, by the *intelligentsia*. They incorporate one of the most beautiful streets in the city, Prechistenka (Kropotkinskaya), which begins at the golden-headed Kremlin and goes on in a straight line to finish at the stunningly beautiful Novodevichy Convent, with its red and white baroque churches and slim, elegant bell-tower.

Even today the streets and lanes around Prechistenka and Vorovsky have an air of superiority and are the setting for many

55A. Zakrevsky Mansion: a ceiling.

foreign embassies. In the sixteenth and seventeenth centuries, the settlements or guilds which provided kitchen and domestic services to the Tsar's court were to be found here. Their names have survived in the streets abutting onto Vorovsky — Khlebny (bread), Stolovy (table), Skatertny (tablecloth), and the old name for Vorovsky itself, Povarskaya (cook). To the south were the settlements concerned with the royal stables Starokonyushenny (Old Stable Lane) and to the west the Khamovniki (weavers). These settlements died a natural death when the Court moved to St Petersburg at the beginning of the eighteenth century and the economic life of the city fell under the sway of merchants and petty traders.

At the end of the eighteenth century when service to the Court was no longer obligatory, many aristocratic families set up residence in Moscow. The Boulevards, which came into being at the end of the eighteenth century replacing the old walls of Bely Gorod, were ideal for the popular pastime of promenading. Many of the fine classical mansions which were built along the tree-lined corridor still survive.

Tolstoy's *War and Peace* contains many references to this part of Moscow. At the top of Vorovsky Street where the Writers' Union now has its headquarters is the large classical mansion which was the prototype for the Rostov family home. Pierre Bezukhov, in some respects drawn from Tolstoy himself, wandered around the Arbat area watching the Fire rage and the French soldiers looting and terrifying the local populace. The tremendous pride in having vanquished the invincible Napoleon helped in finding the funds and energy to rebuild the devastated city. The more domestic, prettier houses of the late classical or Russian Empire like the Zakrevsky Mansion, now used by the Greek Embassy, were officially encouraged and hundreds of similar houses were built in this district.

These houses were to witness the heated arguments over Russia's future by the young men, officers and nobles, who were to become the Decembrists, those who on the cold morning of 14 December 1825 in St Petersburg challenged the right of Nicholas I to take the throne. They were the doomed generation, the golden youth, who would be exiled to Siberia for thirty years.

The western district of old Moscow, between the Boulevards and the Garden Ring, has been a favourite home for many noted Russian writers. Gogol lived on the Boulevards, Chekhov and Bulgakov on the Garden Ring, Pushkin, after his marriage, on the Arbat, Gorky in the fantastic Art Nouveau house by Shekhtel, Tolstoy beyond the Garden Ring in the less fashionable factory district. In modern times the poet and balladist, Bulat Okudzhava, lives near the Arbat which he has celebrated in poetry and song. This intellectual feature of the Arbat continued even after the Revolution when, from the 1920s to 50s, colonies of university professors, scientists, writers and musicians settled in the crowded communal apartments and mansions of the pre-Revolutionary bourgeoisie. However, the leading avant-garde architect of the 20s, Konstantin Melnikov, was able to design and live near the Arbat in his own, incomparable, cylindrical house.

Some of the turn-of-the-century big houses are outstanding architectural creations like the most original of Shekhtel's huge output — the Ryabushinsky Mansion (where Gorky lived) and the Derozhinskaya Mansion. Fortunately the exciting interiors of these houses have mostly survived and are excellently maintained. The gloomier Gothic of Shekhtel's earlier period is also well represented by the Morozov Mansion with its extraordinary entrance hall and finely crafted reception rooms. Many of the other buildings of this period are eclectic in design like the Berg Mansion, now the Italian Embassy, and the House of Friendship, built by yet another member of the large Morozov clan, where every room is richly decorated in different, contrasting styles.

The intellectual cast of western Moscow is evident in the numbers of educational and cultural buildings to be found there: the old University, the Pushkin Museum of Fine Arts (1912), the Lenin Library (1929-40) and the Conservatory and Tchaikovsky Concert Halls. The Conservatory opened in its present building in 1898 when musical development was at its peak in Russia. Tchaikovsky had only recently died, Scriabin, Rimsky-Korsakov, Rachmaninov were in their prime and many other composers were enriching the Russian musical tradition, continued later by the great twentieth-century composers – especially Stravinsky, Prokofiev and Shostakovich.

Great changes were wrought on this part of Moscow after the Revolution. The new Soviet leadership was intent on building monumental projects to the glory of the first socialist state. One such project, the Palace of Soviets, was to be built on the site of the Cathedral of the Redeemer, erected as a memorial to the victory over Napoleon but only completed in 1883. The cathedral, of huge proportions, which dominated the river site and even the cathedrals and palaces of the Kremlin, was blown up in 1931. However, construction of the Palace of Soviets, which was to be the tallest building in the world, encountered severe problems of flooding and with the outbreak of the Second World War the grotesque plan was abandoned. Finally, in 1960, a large outdoor, heated swimming-pool, open even in winter, was built in its place.

Another grandiose scheme of the notorious 1935 General Plan for Moscow involved the construction of a major highway from the gates of the Kremlin, which would benefit the leadership intent on fast transport to their country houses to the west of the city. The once delightful Sobachya Ploshchadka (Dog Square) was razed to the ground and high-rise tower blocks erected in its place, completely at odds with the ordinary human scale of the old districts that still exist on each side of the giants. The intellectuals who lived in the area began to find themselves squeezed out from the centre to the faceless dormitory suburbs. The final straw was the transformation of the beloved old street, the Arbat, with its small convenient shops into a noisy, pedestrian zone taken over by buskers, street artists and hawkers.

54B. Tolstoy House: Sophia Andreyevna's sitting-room with her portrait by Valentin Serov on the left.

54C. Tolstoy House: the master's study where he received guests.

· 54 ·

THE TOLSTOY HOUSE

In the second half of the nineteenth century, the district of Khamovniki, situated beyond the Garden Ring Road, had become an area of factories and workers' hovels. It seems strange that Count Lev Tolstoy chose his Moscow residence here. Yet this working-class district was precisely what intrigued and delighted the famous author. His wooden house with the attractive garden is found along a street rutted with potholes and still dominated by two industrial buildings, a brewery and the silk factory, Krasnaya Roza, which were there in Tolstoy's day. In one of his

pamphlets he wrote, 'I live among factories. Every morning at five o'clock a whistle sounds, then a second, third, ten, on and on. This means that the working day has begun for women, children, old people. At eight o'clock another whistle — for the half-hour break; at twelve a third for the lunch hour and at eight the fourth to announce the end of the working day.'

Tolstoy moved to this unfashionable area in 1882 when he was fifty-four years old, and spent nearly twenty winters here until in 1901 he retired to his estate. He was at the height of his fame for his two outstanding novels, *War and Peace* and *Anna Karenina*. But his residence in this house coincided with the great moral watershed of his life. It was at this time that he experienced his conversion to the new, rational Christianity which he founded

and which eventually led to his excommunication from the Orthodox Church. He also attempted to forswear the revenue from his earlier novels which caused a deep rift with his wife, Sophia Andreyevna.

The high, carved, wooden fence protecting the property from the plebeian neighbourhood still stands with 'LT' carved along the top. The wooden-frame house on two floors, painted a dark, chocolate brown, was built in the 1840s, but was considerably enlarged for the large Tolstoy family in the 1880s. Although a small, unpretentious house for someone of Tolstoy's standing, it had sixteen rooms with several living-in servants. It must seem spacious to today's Muscovites with their average two-room flat. Curiously, it has never been properly wired and can be very dark inside on winter days,

55B. Zakrevsky Mansion: in the drawing-room the heavy acanthus leaves hide earlier mouldings.

particularly the narrow corridor on the first floor where the children had their rooms – the 'catacombs' as they called it. Yet, the lack of electric light combined with the original furnishings and personal belongings allows one to step easily back into Tolstoy's world of the late nineteenth century.

When Tolstoy died at Astapovo in 1910 at the age of eighty-two, pitifully running away from his country estate, Yasnaya Polyana, his widow, Sophia Andreyevna, gave this house, complete with its contents, to the Moscow City Council to be formed into a museum. After the Revolution, in 1920, Lenin confirmed its status and it remains one of the most delightful of the many Moscow museums devoted to outstanding personalities.

····································
· 55 ·
····································

THE ZAKREVSKY MANSION
(THE GREEK EMBASSY)

····································

Foreign embassies are fortunate because they occupy some of the best buildings in Moscow; elegant houses of aristocrats and extravagant mansions of wealthy merchants. The Greeks have been particularly lucky for their embassy is located on a quiet central street in one of the most attractive Empire classical houses of the post-1812 period. It was built in 1818 for a Guards Captain, N.G. Volkov, after severe damage in the 1812 Fire during Napoleon's sojourn in Moscow.

In the middle of the nineteenth century the mansion became the property of Agrafena Zakrevskaya, wife of the notorious Moscow Governor-General, Count Arseny Zakrevsky. Poorly educated and narrow in his views, he was appointed Governor-General in 1848 by Nicholas I who was nervous, in that year of revolutions throughout Europe, of the prospect of any opposition to the regime. Zakrevsky, who held the post for eleven years, proved to be Moscow's most reactionary and tyrannical Governor-General. He regarded even a dinner in a private house as a potential hotbed of dissent and his spies operated everywhere. Under the new, more liberal Tsar, Alexander II, Zakrevsky could not believe that the incipient campaign for the liberation of the serfs could possibly be a serious development supported by the Court. At odds with the times Zakrevsky, in 1859, was relieved of his duties.

His wife, Agrafena, was a remarkable hostess and outstanding personality of the era. A beautiful woman, she reputedly dallied with leading members of the literary world. In the 1820s, the golden age of Russian poetry, Agrafena had a long affair with the romantic poet and friend of Pushkin, Yevgeny Baratynsky, who describes her in his lyrical poem, 'The Ball'. Pushkin himself knew Agrafena and there is some evidence that the poet had an affair with her in 1828. She is thought by some to be the prototype for the brilliant 'Nina Voronskaya, that Cleopatra of the Neva' in chapter eight, verse XVI of Pushkin's *Eugene Onegin*.

The house is quintessentially Russian Empire with its fine portico of twelve Doric columns and discreet mouldings facing the courtyard. Inside a splendid ceiling light illuminates a noble staircase that divides in two, leading to the main reception rooms. Facing the landing is a portrait by K. Gun of the German mistress of the house who was responsible for its fundamental redesign in the 1880s. The ebullient ceiling plasterwork of the salon of that time obscures the earlier, more restrained mouldings. However the 1818 interior order of rooms was not affected by the 1880 alterations and the enfilade of reception rooms on the courtyard side remains original. Among the finest features of the house are the artificial marble stoves that seem to organically unite floor and ceiling.

55C. Zakrevsky Mansion: an alcove off the stairwell with the Gun portrait.

56A. Ryabushinsky Mansion: the sinuous form of the staircase turns and twists in ascent.

THE RYABUSHINSKY MANSION (THE GORKY MUSEUM)

The name of Fyodor Shekhtel recurs constantly in any assessment of the achievements of Moscow architecture of the turn of the century. Shekhtel is not only the greatest Russian architect of Art Nouveau (or 'Moderne' as the Russians call it), but stands on a par with any of the great architects of the genre in western Europe (his style would seem to be closest to the Belgian, Victor Horta). In 1900 he designed and built at the Nikitsky Gate the most perfect Art Nouveau house in Moscow, the mansion for Stepan Ryabushinsky.

The Ryabushinskys were one of the top twenty-five Moscow merchant families. Deeply involved with city government they were, with their immense wealth, influential in publishing, art collecting and philanthropy. Stepan Ryabushinsky was a third-generation descendant from the peasantry and, like many of the leading merchant families, a strict Old Believer. He was, at twenty-six, head of the trading side of the family business; his main occupation, however, was as a discriminating collector of icons, the earliest form of Russian art which, at that time, was only

B

C

56. Ryabushinsky Mansion: B: the limestone staircase with bronze and glass lamp forms the focus of the house. C: the water theme reflected in the waves and droplets of the stained-glass window.

beginning to be appreciated. Thus he commissioned this outstanding house not only as his home, but as the setting for his icon collection. Art Nouveau and icons, one would think, were at odds with each other, but in a surprising way the graceful curving lines of the saints in their strong, primary colours blended most harmoniously with the undulations and strong features of the architecture.

The house, set back in its own grounds,

still has the capacity to astonish when encountered suddenly from the quiet ochre-coloured streets of nineteenth-century Moscow. No two windows alike, bulging porches with flat roofs, the colour, pinkish glazed brick offset by the gold of the window casings, all serve to enhance the drama of the house, the whole effect harmonious and stimulating.

Inside the arrangement is surprisingly domestic with modest-sized rooms

56D. Ryabushinsky Mansion: the finely crafted doors of the salon/library.

grouped around a central stairwell. But the staircase is the dominant feature of the house, executed in the fluidity of line that is so fundamental to Art Nouveau. The newel post in Italian limestone resembles marble and is strangely warm to the touch. It curves and twists resolving its agony in a lamp dripping with stalactites; the staircase then proceeds upwards in majestic curves with unexpected apertures, like

kneaded dough, to be met at the top by another post formed by writhing snakes. Water is the dominant theme; waves are in the design of the parquet flooring, drop-like circles decorate the stained-glass window and the ceiling of the dining-room represents an underwater kingdom.

After the Revolution the Ryabushinskys went abroad and, in 1931, the house became the home of the writer, Maxim

Gorky. It seems incongruous that the great 'proletarian' writer should be given the home of a fabulously wealthy merchant, the class he so often satirized. Long a sufferer from tuberculosis, he died suddenly in 1936, before the worst excesses of Stalin's reign of terror which was to prove fatal for so many writers. A museum to Gorky has been established in this remarkable house.

56E. Ryabushinsky Mansion: originally the salon, later Gorky's library.

· 57 ·

THE BERG MANSION
(THE ITALIAN EMBASSY)

The imposing Berg Mansion with its jut-
ting porch, forbidding in dark sandstone,
seems to brood over the street but its
uninviting exterior is belied by the fantastic and richly adorned interior. It illustrates
the true meaning of eclecticism; so many
architectural styles are represented within
that it is hard to realize that one is still in
the same building. The magnificent Gothic
hall that rises the whole height of the
building to be lit from the roof leads to a
huge square salon with ceiling paintings
and a frieze in the baroque manner framed
by mouldings in gold and artificial marble
pilasters. The hanging light fittings are
skilfully worked in an Art Nouveau
manner using metalwork and bulbous
mother-of-pearl for the lighting panels.
The whole effect would be too much if it
were not for the less resplendent walls
decorated only by the pilasters and
sconces.

Ringed around the central main hall is a

*57. Berg Mansion: A: doorway into the master
bedroom. B: the spacious drawing-room with
painted ceiling, frieze and unusual lamp.*

57. Berg Mansion: C: the Art Nouveau bedroom ceiling and lamp.
D: a view of the ceiling of the white marble entrance hall.

series of rooms, one of which leads to the main bedroom decorated in swirling Art Nouveau. A nearby narrow storage section has cupboards also in the style of Art Nouveau. Opening onto the garden is the medieval dining-room with its wooden panelled ceiling and wainscotting. Every-

where there are superb mahogany doors with large brass hinges and fine original furniture. The classical period is represented in this wealth of architecture only by the front vestibule.

The house was built in 1897 by a well-known Moscow architect, P.S. Boitsev, for

57E. Berg Mansion: the Gothic great hall.

the textile and wrought-iron manu-facturer, Baron S.P. Berg. The Bergs were obliged to leave the house after the Revolu-tion when it was confiscated and given to the Embassy of Germany. The Bolsheviks had just signed the humiliating Peace of Brest-Litovsk (March 1918) giving up a huge part of Russia's territories in the west to obtain peace with the Germans. The Left Socialist Revolutionaries, allies of the Bolsheviks during the Revolution, agitated fiercely against the peace treaty and on 6 July two of their number brazenly marched into the house and killed the German Ambassador, Count Wilhelm von Mirbach, in the main hall. This was the signal for uprisings in Moscow, Petrograd and Yaroslavl, but within a few days the Bolshevik forces managed to contain the disturbances. Lenin hurried to the gloomy house to extend his apologies and condo-lences in person.

Offices of the Communist International then occupied the Berg House until 1924 when it became the Italian Embassy. The superb condition of its interior is due to their care.

57F. Berg Mansion: the dining-room looking on to the conservatory.

58A. Derozhinskaya Mansion: the central staircase illustrating the tree and plant theme.

· 58 ·

THE DEROZHINSKAYA
MANSION
(THE AUSTRALIAN EMBASSY)

Fyodor Shekhtel's second Art Nouveau masterpiece, built in 1901, is contemporaneous with the Ryabushinsky Mansion. The two freely designed houses are quite individual sharing only the great artistry and imagination with which they are executed and the use of finely crafted materials, especially the rich variety of woods. Whereas the Ryabushinsky Mansion is made up of small rooms on a cosy, domestic scale, the Derozhinskaya Mansion, composed of one immense, baronial hall surrounded by lesser rooms, is more austere. In its simplicity and lack of adornment it is a step on the way to Shekhtel's next stage, that of rational Art Nouveau.

The grand hall, 12 cubic metres, reaches almost the full height of the house. Wall panelling takes up half the height of the room which, with the wooden coffered ceiling, helps to offset the unbearable feeling of height and size. Nevertheless, there is still the impression that everything is designed for giants. The wooden surround of the fireplace which rises above the panelling is also of gigantic stature. The proportions are absolutely correct, but the dimensions are uncomfortable; the human form is too small for the room.

Although the ornamentation is sparse it reflects two superbly executed themes. Stylized trees are carved over the fireplace, in the library gallery and on the main staircase. A simple but wonderfully effective design of rotating triangles appears in the brass door furniture, on the fireplace and elsewhere in the house. They occur, too, in the design of the original furnishings also created by Shekhtel. From original photographs it seems the seating arrangements in the grand hall were like hanging settees attached to the panelling; there was little furniture and the floor covering was bare parquet. Although the architecture of the house seems so unyielding, it was built to a high standard of

58. Derozhinskaya Mansion: B: the library with gallery decorated with carved trees. C: finely designed central heating vents.

B

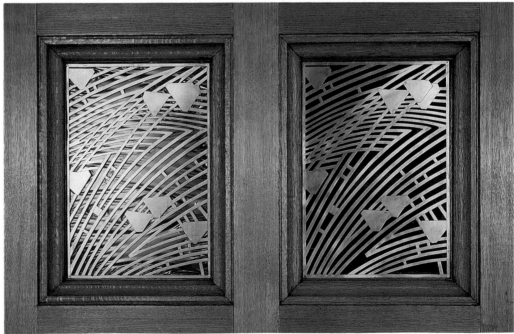

C

58. Derozhinskaya Mansion: D: guest bedroom with original ceiling lights.
E: brass door handle demonstrating the rotating triangles design.

comfort and convenience; the central heating system was hidden within ducts in the walls. The lighting is also most original; hanging on brass chains in the grand hall or hidden within the ceiling in the guest bedroom or part of the newel post on the main staircase.

Alexandra Derozhinskaya was the daughter of a textile manufacturer whose factory was in the neighbourhood; the house was a gift to her on her wedding to the manager of the factory. One wonders how she liked the strange house. After the Revolution it became, for a short time, offices for the Commissariat of Education where Nadezhda Krupskaya, Lenin's wife, worked. By the late 1920s it was at the disposal of the Foreign Ministry and housed a bewildering number of missions including the Chinese, until, in 1959, it became the home of the Australian Embassy.

58F. Derozhinskaya Mansion: the great hall with outsize fireplace embellished with stylized trees.

THE MELNIKOV HOUSE

On a small lane near the Arbat is a remarkable cylindrical house situated in its own garden. On the crown of the façade the words, 'Konstantin Melnikov Architect', are boldly inscribed. The strange house and rare garden were built to his own design by Konstantin Melnikov, one of the most original avant-garde architects of the post-Revolution period when the Soviet Union became the world leader in modern architecture. His Soviet pavilion at the 1925 Paris Exhibition was awarded the Grand Prix; sadly none of his more ambitious projects was realized, but eleven buildings designed by him survive in Moscow including five workers' clubs, two bus garages and a market.

The house is composed of two interlocking cylinders, one slightly higher than the other. The plan is deceptively simple; ground and first-floor rooms use partitions instead of solid walls to divide the space. The material is brick with stucco overlaid and within the walls hexagonal apertures are placed at regular intervals so that windows can be closed up or revealed as the owner wishes; the top floor studio, used by his son, is lit evenly by the rhythmically placed hexagonal windows.

Tragically the still relatively young Melnikov who had the world of architecture at his feet became the object of ridicule and contempt in the 1930s as Stalin tightened his grip. Although Melnikov avoided arrest he was never able to practise his profession again and even into the early 1960s he and his work were personally attacked by Khrushchev.

Melnikov died in relative obscurity in 1974. Happily he was never forced to give up his unique house, the only example of an architect in Soviet Moscow living in a house of his own design. Recognition and fame have belatedly come and thanks to the devoted efforts of his son, the artist Victor Melnikov, the house is to become a museum in his name and is to undergo much needed repairs. In 1990 Melnikov's centenary was officially celebrated and given wide publicity in the Soviet Union.

59. Melnikov House: the architect's son, Victor, in his top-floor studio.

60. Writers' Union: the dining hall with modern stained-glass windows.

· 60 ·

THE WRITERS' UNION

The headquarters and club of the Soviet Writers' Union is entered via a most unprepossessing 1950s building of yellow brick on Herzen Street. It links up, however, with an old mansion that faces the parallel road, Vorovsky Street, and which provides accommodation for the club's meeting rooms and splendid dining hall where the excellent cuisine is greatly appreciated in a city notoriously poor in restaurants.

The picturesque house with its porch and steeply pitched roofs was built in 1887 by the architect P.S. Boitsov on one of Moscow's most fashionable streets. The owner, Prince Svyatopolk-Chetvertinsky, acquired the land from the neighbouring large estate of Baron Bode-Kolychev, whose large classical mansion next door (also now used by the Writers' Union) is thought to be the prototype for the Rostov family home in Tolstoy's *War and Peace*. By the time of the Revolution the house was owned by Countess Olsufyeva by whose name it is generally known. The interior is finished largely in wood, originally stained black. However, in the 1960s the leadership of the union decided the black panelling (and staircase) of the dining hall, with its huge chandelier, was too oppressive and went to some trouble and expense to have the wood stripped and stained a honey colour. Nevertheless, the panelling of the high ceiling, perhaps too difficult to reach, remains black and forms an awkward contrast. The tall stained-glass windows in the corner of the hall-cum-restaurant were similarly vandalized; tasteless modern design replaces the original glass.

After 1917 it became a nursery school at first, and then, in 1932, the home of the Writers' Union which was set up in that same year. All writers were corralled into one organization strictly controlled by the Party. The history of the union since then has not been an uplifting one. Writers of the calibre of Akhmatova, Zoshchenko, Pasternak and Solzhenitsyn were expelled, and talented writers denied membership even in recent times, while literary hacks enjoyed the privileges of membership which include guaranteed publication, summer homes, holidays, special medical treatment and trips abroad. The Writers'

Union seems to be almost the last cultural organization to mend its ways in the era of *glasnost*, although there are signs of a new liberalism more in keeping with the times. President Reagan's televised address at the union during his visit in May 1988 on freedom of the written word made a considerable impact. Typically, however, the union leadership decked out its headquarters for the occasion in the manner of the Potemkin villages with fine furniture borrowed from other institutions which, on the day after Reagan's visit, lined the corridors waiting to be returned.

· 61 ·

THE PUSHKIN MUSEUM

Like the British Museum the Pushkin Museum is executed in the classical style with huge pediment, portico in the Ionic order, and frieze depicting the Olympic Games. The museum was the dream-child of Ivan Tsvetayev, Professor of Classics at the University of Moscow and Director of the Rumyantsev Museum, whose daughter, Marina, was a remarkable poetess. The museum was funded by private means, two-thirds of which was donated by Yury Nechaev-Maltsev, the owner of the famous crystal factory at Gusev, east of Moscow. Tsvetayev, the son of a poor priest who had made it to the top of the university ladder, was able to realize his dream of establishing a museum of sculpture and architectural fragments. He and his wife spent many years collecting and cataloguing plaster casts of sculpture from all over the western world.

The building was to the design of P. S. Boitsov, but it was executed by Roman Klein, one of Moscow's most respected and energetic builders of the late nineteenth and early twentieth centuries. Within, the museum is divided into spacious courts, and on the upper floor a fine Corinthian basilica is situated where special exhibitions and concerts are held. The powerful main staircase, lined on the first floor by columns, was designed by Ivan Zholtovsky, the committed classical architect, who during his long career never deviated to Art Nouveau or Constructivism, but remained faithful to the Italian Renaissance and Palladio. Because of financial problems and a fire, the

61. Pushkin Museum: the Zholtovsky staircase lined with marble Ionic columns.

museum took fourteen years to build but, at last, on a sunny May day in 1912 it was officially opened. Nicholas II with his wife and little daughters arrived to officiate; the grand duchesses were described by Marina Tsvetayeva as 'a cloud of white butterflies, an enchanting cloud . . .' and her father as standing 'under the very pediment of the museum, at the zenith of his life . . .'

In 1924 a gallery for paintings and engravings was set up as the museum began to acquire paintings from the fabulous private collections so assiduously gathered together before the Revolution by the Moscow merchants Sergei Shchukin, Ivan Morozov, Vsevolod Girshman, and many others. Its name was changed from the Alexander III Museum of Fine Art to the Pushkin Museum of Fine Art. After the war the collections were shared with the Hermitage in Leningrad and with many provincial museums. Even so it has a wealth of fine paintings, as well as the sculpture and artifacts from Egypt and the Mediterranean world, and it has taken its place as one of the world's outstanding museums.

· 62 ·

THE HOUSE OF FRIENDSHIP

The House of Friendship is one of the idiosyncratic Moscow mansions built for the nouveau-riche third- and fourth-generation merchants at the end of the nineteenth century. It looks like a Moorish castle with its round turrets and lace-like crown; there is a curious maritime theme of twisted ropes and sea shells clinging to the walls.

The mansion was built in 1898 by V. Mazyrin for one of the younger sons of the Morozov clan, Arseny Abramovich. The Morozov line began in the early nineteenth century with Savva Morozov who started a textile factory after the Fire of 1812 during Napoleon's invasion. His four sons divided the business between them, each remaining independent from the other; the Abram line inherited the Tverskaya textile factory. By the late nineteenth century, with the opening of the

62A. House of Friendship: dried flowers complement the marble fireplace in the niche.

C

62. House of Friendship: B: the white room used for receptions. C: a detail of the ceiling.

market to Asia after the completion of the trans-Siberian railway, textiles were a rapidly expanding market where large fortunes were made.

Arseny's mother, Varvara, was a blue-stocking famous for her interest in and support for education for women and for the working classes; she founded special courses and schools. Her second husband, whom she could not legally marry owing to a clause in her first husband's will, was V. M. Sobolev, who was the publisher of the popular and influential newspaper,

Russkiye Vedomosti. They lived next door to their son and must have been shocked at his exhibitionist behaviour and unorthodox taste.

The mansion is loosely based on the sixteenth-century Casa de la Conchas in Salamanca which Arseny had seen on his travels. His character matched the extravagant façade of the house; known for his wild parties and high living he once shot himself in the foot to see if he could bear the pain. Unfortunately, this caused his death from blood poisoning aged only

E

62. House of Friendship: D: a ceiling detail of the auditorium. E: the auditorium and concert hall.

twenty-four which no doubt further distressed his admirable mother and stepfather.

If the façade facing the main avenue is eccentric in the extreme, the interior is more like other Moscow mansions in having a wealth of contrasting rooms executed in different styles as the whim of the architect and patron dictated. There are fine woods for ceilings and doors, gold-leaf figures and ornament, a marble Greco-Roman room with Ionic columns supporting a gallery, a mad fireplace in the main hall with intricate leaves in superbly wrought plasterwork and on the chimney-breast a stylized forest of mounted hunters and game. The painted and plastered ceilings are in remarkably good condition as indeed is the rest of the house.

In early 1918 the mansion shared the fate of many other grand houses in Moscow when it was occupied by anarchists who were eventually flushed out by the Cheka (secret police) four months later. Soon afterwards Proletkult, an experimental organization whose aim was to replace bourgeois culture with a new,

working-class culture, commandeered the house. The poets, Vladimir Mayakovsky and Sergei Yesenin, helped set up discussion groups and the theatre and film directors, Vsevolod Meyerhold and Sergei Eisenstein, staged dramas. Following the invasion of the Soviet Union by Hitler's troops in June 1941, the British information journal, *Britansky Soyuznik*, was published here until the end of the war.

In the 1950s the mansion became the headquarters of the Society for Cultural Relations with Foreign Countries known, since 1959, as the House of Friendship. Here relations with official foreign visitors were institutionalized and controlled; groups would be invited to watch Russian folk dancing or to have stilted discussions with Soviet writers and cultural bureaucrats. Its role may well change in the new conditions prevailing in the Soviet Union. Likewise plans to build a huge, cylindrical House of Peace and People's Friendship opposite – which would have involved the demolition of some fine houses including No.9 originally built by Tolstoy's grandfather – seem to have been shelved.

62F. House of Friendship: the marble room in Greek style is the most richly appointed.

62G. *House of Friendship: the fanciful fireplace is the focal point of the main hall.*

THE GLEBOV HOUSE

Facing the Pushkin Museum from a side-street and offsetting its monumentality with a more intimate form, is a charming house of the post-Napoleonic period. A fine example of Russian Empire with its Ionic columns, semicircular attic window, balcony and discrete medallions of musicians framed by horns of plenty, the Glebov House was built in 1826 by Fyodor Shestakov, one of the finest classical architects, who helped to rebuild Moscow after its destruction in the 1812 Fire.

The mild exterior does not prepare one for the disturbing décor of the interior hall and stairwell. Strange dancing figures, half animal half man without hands or feet, line the walls in strips repeated in incomprehensible patterns as if in code. On the wall three false doors are painted without handles or hinges. Rings of hieroglyphs circle the ceiling with a large star at the centre and strange globes surmounted by crosses at the corners. Swans support the world. All these odd symbols suggest Freemasonry. The Masonic movement had arrived in Russia in the eighteenth century where it found fertile ground among the nobility and intellectuals, particularly in Moscow where it took the form of mild opposition to the Court. Empress Catherine regarded its exponents with deep suspicion and on occasion even had them imprisoned. Some of the leading conspirators in the Decembrist revolt of 1825 were Freemasons.

It is not clear when the interior paintings were done although the most likely date suggested is the middle of the nineteenth century in the reign of Nicholas I. The first owner, Glebov, died the year the house was finished and his widow let it to various well-known families; the Golitsyns, Musin-Pushkins and Khan Tarkovsky. In the late nineteenth century it was purchased by Buryshkin, the textile merchant, who was passionately interested in the history of Moscow. With his collection of documents and artifacts he turned his house into something resembling the first Museum of Moscow; he had intended to

63. *Glebov House: the mysterious staircase decorated with masonic symbols.*

64A. Lenin Library: the well-used third reading room is lit from two sides.

leave his collection to such a museum to be called 'Old Moscow'. Buryshkin left Russia after the Revolution and his collection eventually went to the Museum of the History and Reconstruction of Moscow (now the Museum of the History of Moscow). The house shared the fate of so many fine private homes and was converted to communal apartments with one family per room. In 1965 it was taken over by the Pushkin Museum to house its extensive collection of engravings and drawings; it was during the extensive renovation carried out by the museum that the curious paintings were revealed.

· 64 ·

THE LENIN LIBRARY

The Lenin Library with over 30 million books is the main Soviet library and the depository for all published material in the USSR. The new building, which took over twenty years to complete, reflects the evolution of Soviet architecture from the stark simplicity of the avant-garde of the 1920s to the full-blown decorative style of Soviet classicism of the 1940s and 50s.

The library was meant to harmonize with the majesty of the predominantly classical eighteenth/nineteenth-century architecture of the surrounding buildings, in particular the old Lenin Library next door, the Pashkov House, Bazhenov's masterpiece of the 1780s, situated on a promontory overlooking the Kremlin. The winners of the 1927 competition for the library were Vladimir Shchuko and Vladimir Gelfreikh, two of the leading architects of Soviet classicism. They envisaged a building with a colonnade at its entrance bare of adornment or capital. This cold exterior, although criticized by the constructivists, was not totally at odds with their theory of functionalism combined with beauty of form. Commenced in 1929, its first stage was not completed before 1941 and some of the interior work was only finished in the 1950s. In the course of this long building period, the library was increasingly encrusted with sculpture and reliefs as it came under the influence of the monumental neo-classicism of the Palace of the Soviets, under construction (but never completed) on the nearby Kropotkinskaya Embank-

ment. Thus, over the years, the original concept for the library became perverted.

Inside, the library opens up with an ostentatious grand marble staircase leading up to the catalogues and four main reading rooms. The spacious reading rooms, which can hold over 300 readers, are well lit and airy although with two people to a desk a little crowded. In winter, entrance is regulated by the quaint system of queuing for the cloakroom where all the available hooks are soon filled. Foreigners are particularly privileged as they are allowed to use the First Reading Room, reserved for university teachers, those with doctorates and people of distinction.

With the advent of *glasnost*, books in the *spetskhran* (special depository) are now being made available to everyone; among these forbidden books were a large proportion of the library's foreign publications.

The library suffered a great blow in 1985 when a new metro station, the Borovitskaya, opened underneath its huge depository causing cracks and the loss of some 40,000 books. The beautiful Pashkov Mansion which had stood for two centuries was also badly damaged provoking a vigorous campaign in the Press against the planners and the metro builders. Repairs will be carried out with the help of French contractors, but will necessarily take a long time and there are fears that the library will have to close for part of this period.

64B. Lenin Library: the main staircase with catalogues to right and left.

65A. Stanislavsky House: the dining-room with traditional white covers on the furniture.

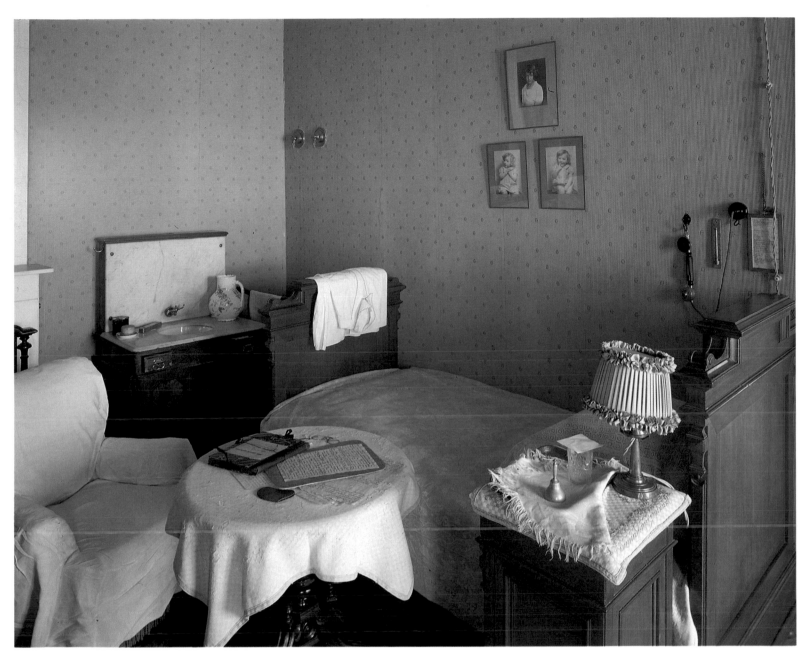

65B. *Stanislavsky House: the master's bedroom with photographs of his wife and daughters.*

· 65 ·

THE STANISLAVSKY HOUSE

From Stanislavsky Street the old house appears to be deceptively small, but from the back it is clear that it is more substantial, with three floors. The vaulted ground floor is of the late seventeenth century, the rest dating from the middle of the eighteenth when it belonged to P.S. Khlopov, a captain of the Izmailovsky Regiment. During the sojourn of the Khlopov family the fine interior was decorated. The ceilings with their precise stylized border paintings in tempera of flora and fauna are among the

best of the period to be found in Moscow.

In 1921 part of the old house was given, as his residence and studio, to Konstantin Stanislavsky, then aged fifty-eight, the great actor-director and founder of method acting and the Moscow Arts Theatre. Stanislavsky, a member of the rich merchant family, the Alekseyevs, was already residing in a fine house of his own, but it was requisitioned as a chauffeurs' club. Lunacharsky, the minister for the Enlightenment in the first Bolshevik government, was able to persuade Lenin that Stanislavsky should have a reasonably good apartment. Nevertheless, Stanislavsky and his family did not have the whole house but only the first floor; other families occupied the ground and top floors.

The charming apartment has a large hall with a raised floor and columns at one end which lent itself to rehearsals when Stanislavsky was not well enough to go to the theatre. From this hall is a corridor off which are various domestic rooms; Stanislavsky's study, the bedroom and dressing-room of his wife, Maria Lilina (also an actress), the dining-room and Stanislavsky's bedroom. All the furniture is original.

The house was visited by Stanislavsky's students, actors and writers of the famous plays at the Arts Theatre. Mikhail Bulgakov was a frequent guest at the time his play, *The White Guard*, was in rehearsal; he had many disagreements with the great director. Set in Kiev, it was the first play to deal

66A. Savva Morozov Mansion: the carved stone fireplace of the dining-room.

realistically with a family sympathetic to the Whites in the upheaval of the Revolution. Surprisingly, it became Stalin's favourite play and thus helped to save Bulgakov in the dark days of the 1930s.

Stanislavsky, who died in 1938, must have been appalled at the events of the reign of terror unleashed by Stalin in 1937; his former student and colleague, Meyerhold, was to be among its countless victims. Although the great director was canonized after his death, the style of acting he introduced degenerated into dull, dogmatized realism during the Stalin period and his theatre, the Moscow Arts Theatre, likewise stagnated. Stanislavsky's daughters helped organize the museum which was opened in 1948 and is administered by the Moscow Arts Theatre.

· 66 ·

THE SAVVA MOROZOV MANSION

Fyodor Shekhtel, who became the genius of Art Nouveau in Moscow, constructed his first city mansion in 1893-8 for Savva Morozov, the most outstanding member of the Morozov clan of textile barons. It was one of the first Moscow mansions in a freely interpreted Gothic style, with square and round towers, turrets, pointed windows and lace-like finishes at roof level. The entrance hall continues the Gothic theme of the exterior with a vengeance in a wonderful display of wood, bronze and

brass, superbly lit from a large south-facing window which looks out onto the garden terrace. A fantastic dragon within the staircase twists its head around to threaten the intruder. The whole effect is not unlike a stage set for some Transylvanian horror story relieved only by the profusion of light everywhere.

To the left of the main hall is a panelled dining-room dominated by a great stone carved fireplace. The other principal reception rooms lead off to the right. The magnificent ballroom with superb parquet flooring leads into two salons, one Gothic, one rococo, parallel to the ballroom. The work of Mikhail Vrubel, the finest artist of the period, who often worked with Shekhtel, is also represented in painted panels and a stained-glass window.

66B. Savva Morozov Mansion: the fantastic Gothic entrance hall with outsize window.

66C. Savva Morozov Mansion: the spacious white ballroom with original chandelier.

Shekhtel. After the Revolution, it was used as the centre for organizing relief for the Volga famine. The Ministry of Foreign Affairs, who are the present landlords and maintain the house to a high standard, hold official receptions here, an appropriate use for this striking house.

· 67 ·

METRO KIEVSKAYA

Kiev Railway Station was built in 1913-20 by Ivan Rerberg in a fine monumental classical style that blends in well with Soviet neo-classicism. It has an amazingly functional railway shed of glass and iron with an unusually broad span designed by Vladimir Shukhov, the engineer responsible for the glass roof of GUM twenty years earlier. The railway provides services to the south to the Crimea and south-west to the Ukraine. It is served by three metro lines. The first on the Filyovskaya Line was built in 1937 by architect Dmitry Chechulin. This short, shallow line, made up of only four stations, brought travellers from the Kremlin walls to Kiev Station, providing a quick passage via the suburban trains to the dachas of the leadership at a time when they did not all have cars.

The second, opened in 1953 on the Arbatsko-Pokrovskaya Line, linked up with earlier stations in eastern Moscow that were constructed during the war.

The florid décor of the third station on the splendid Circle Line, opened in 1954, is typical of the late Stalin period (he died in 1953, but architectural styles did not change until later). The hall is dominated by large mosaic panels with elaborate frames on the theme of Russian Ukrainian friendship. The panels, by A.V. Mysin, depict such subjects as 'Pushkin in the Ukraine' and 'Lenin Proclaims Soviet Government'. A large mosaic portrait of Lenin on the end wall completes the picture. Today these naïve representations have a hollow look, particularly after the disaster at Chernobyl when tens of thousands of panic-stricken refugees from the Ukraine poured into Moscow and the metro stations were choked for weeks.

The patron for whom Shekhtel designed this strange but exciting mansion was Savva Morozov, whose wife, a former factory girl in the Morozov textile mills, seems to have enjoyed the singular mansion more than her husband (it was registered in her name). He preferred a more simple life and his study on the first floor was markedly bare of ornament in contrast to her florid apartments. Morozov, a third-generation industrial magnate, was sympathetic to the revolutionary movement. He was a close friend of the writer Maxim Gorky and helped to secure his release from prison; he even gave money to Lenin to publish his newspaper, *Iskra*. He was also passionately interested in the theatre and rescued the Moscow Arts Theatre in 1902 from heavy debts. With his financial and political interests pulling him in opposite directions, the contradictions in his life were such that in 1905, the year of revolution in Russia, he committed suicide while on a visit to Nice.

After Savva Morozov's death the mansion was purchased by Mikhail Ryabushinsky whose brother, Stepan, lived down the road in another mansion by

67. Metro Kievskaya: a mosaic panel on the Circle Line depicting the opening of a hydro-electric station in the Ukraine.

М.И. КАЛИНИН И
Г.К. ОРДЖОНИКИДЗЕ
НА ОТКРЫТИИ
ДНЕПРОГЭСА
1932 г.

68. *Metro Arbatskaya: the arched tunnel opened in 1953.*
69. *Tchaikovsky Concert Hall: Meyerhold's elliptical stage serves well as a concert hall.*

· 68 ·

METRO ARBATSKAYA

The Arbat is a special part of Moscow. The old street was dressed up in 1985, traffic was denied access and it became Moscow's first pedestrian zone, a lively place full of hawkers and artists. At one end, but divided from it by the underpass of the Boulevard, is the unusual metro pavilion for Arbatskaya of the Filyovsky Line which opened in 1935. It is of red brick in the shape of a five-pointed star, a favourite device of Soviet architects of the 1930s, with its name inscribed in fine lower-case lettering. The metro and line are built on the site of a church, Tikhon the Wonder-worker, which, like its neighbouring Church of Saints Boris and Gleb, was demolished in the early 30s.

The second line, Arbatsko-Pokrovskaya, opened in 1953, was set deeper underground. The vestibule, by L.M. Polyakov and Yu. P. Zenkevich, resembles a great arched tunnel with red marble plinths, bronze hanging lamps and ceramic flowers decorating the walls and ceiling. The line links up with Vozdvizhenka, Borovitskaya and Biblioteka im. Lenina, all within a dozen yards of each other. This is the busiest metro interchange in Moscow and it is no wonder that the latest line, the Borovitskaya, was responsible for causing cracks in the Lenin Library situated immediately above.

· 69 ·

THE TCHAIKOVSKY CONCERT HALL

At Mayakovsky Square where it meets Tverskaya (Gorky) Street there is a large rectangular flat-roofed building with a portico and façade like an oriental carpet. Now the Tchaikovsky Concert Hall, its complex history is closely connected to the development of revolutionary theatre in Moscow in the 1920s.

After the Revolution the old Zon Comedy Theatre, which stood on this site, became the home of the theatre of Meyerhold, the brilliant director of the 'biomechanic' athletic method of acting. Here he created his innovative productions, better described as pageants, many with distinct political messages, to which the public were invited free of charge. The conservative-minded Bolshevik leadership barely tolerated these productions, but Lunacharsky, in charge of education and

culture, was adroit in protecting the more experimental aspects of the theatre and artistic world. With the sets designed by such avant-garde artists as Malevich, Popova and Stepanova, productions of Mayakovsky's *The Bedbug* or Gogol's *The Government Inspector*, were unforgettable.

Meyerhold's ingenious plan to rebuild the old Zon Theatre combined stage and public seating in the shape of a large ellipse, the stage protruding into the audience like a long tongue. There were to be no curtains and the orchestra pit was to be at the back of the stage. By 1938 the building was well advanced but, tragically, in the same year Meyerhold, more and more isolated in the growing climate of political repression, suffered the closing of his temporary theatre on Tverskaya (Gorky) Street. A year later he was arrested and died in a Siberian camp; his wife was brutally murdered in her apartment a few days after his arrest.

In 1940 the now defunct Meyerhold Theatre building had been acquired by the Moscow Philharmonia and the architect of socialist realism, Dmitry Chechulin, transformed it into the familiar Soviet classicism with a portico, sculptural bas-reliefs and red and white patterned exterior walls. Inside, in typical Soviet fashion, a winter garden and fountain were added and a large organ was installed in the orchestra space. However, Meyerhold's unusual stage and seating plan survives, a fitting reminder of the great, tragic director.

······························

· 70 ·

······························

THE MOSCOW
CONSERVATORY

······························

The second half of the nineteenth century in Russia saw an unprecedented development in the field of music and the emergence of national composers of the stature of Tchaikovsky, Glinka, Moussorgsky and Borodin. In response to this upsurge of interest, the Moscow Conservatory was founded in 1866 by Nikolai Rubinstein as a school of composition and musicianship; it is now the largest music school in the Soviet Union. The present building of the Conservatory, formerly the eighteenth-century Moscow mansion of Princess Yekaterina Dashkova, friend of Catherine

II and founder of the Russian Academy, was acquired in 1877. Although the plan of the original building was retained, it was entirely rebuilt inside to accommodate the halls and teaching rooms. The architect, V.P. Zagorsky, refused his fee and constructed the marble staircase at his own expense with two of the Morozov family paying for the furniture and the rest paid for by a government grant, public donations and the inheritance left by Rubinstein. The first concert, dedicated to Tchaikovsky who died five years earlier, was held in 1898.

The Conservatory is a much loved institution in Moscow. Since Russia occupies such a strong position in the music field the list of musicians who have been associated with the Conservatory is remarkable; they include Rachmaninov, Scriabin, Shostakovich, Prokofiev and latterly, Shnittke and Gubaidullina. Although the music world has been a relatively sheltered place in the upheavals of Soviet political-cultural life, two major composers, Prokofiev and Shostakovich, did not escape unscathed. In 1948 they were attacked by the Party at the instigation of the notorious Andrei Zhdanov for 'formalism' and were constantly harassed by Stalin's cultural bureaucrats. Prokofiev died in 1953 on the same day as Stalin; Shostakovich continued to compose, sometimes parodying the tenets of socialist realism which the unsuspecting music leadership failed to perceive. Justice scored a macabre triumph when one of his most malevolent chief critics suffered a heart attack and died in the main hall of the Conservatory during the première of a Shostakovich symphony in which the composer expressed his anguish at the years of Stalinist repression.

Softly lit from high windows the elongated hall, which fills the former courtyard, faces the stage with the marvellous organ donated to the Conservatory by S.P. Von Derviz as its backdrop. Along the walls are fourteen portraits of famous composers including, in addition to the major Russian composers, Bach and Beethoven. In 1940 four of the original portraits – Handel, Haydn, Mendelsson and Gluck – were replaced by Moussorgsky, Rimsky-Korsakov, Dargomyzhsky and Chopin; presumably it had been decided that where possible Slavs should replace Germans.

······························

70. *Moscow Conservatory: medallions of famous composers flank the stage.*

71. Bulgakov Staircase: graffiti on the theme of the devil.

· 71 ·

THE BULGAKOV STAIRCASE

A phenomenon in Moscow in recent years has been the popularity of the novel by Mikhail Bulgakov, *The Master and Margarita*. References to its characters constantly appear in literature and a play, a film and even a ballet have been based on it. The cult nature of the public admiration for it would have astonished Bulgakov; the novel was only published twenty-five years after his death. He began the magnificent satire on life in the Soviet Union in 1928. By the middle of the 30s the political climate was such that Bulgakov was no longer able to publish and his request to be allowed to emigrate was turned down personally by Stalin who, ironically, was a great admirer of his earlier work. Although very ill, Bulgakov just managed to complete *The Master and Margarita* a few days before his death in March 1940. His widow was obliged to hide the manuscript and it was not published until the late 60s. Its immense success in the 80s stems partly from the wonderfully produced play of the novel put on by Yuri Lyubimov at the Taganka Theatre; it was taken off the repertoire when Lyubimov left but since his return has been resurrected.

What is it about this novel that inspires such adoration? Bulgakov, in alternating sardonic and grotesque passages, highlights the absurdities and injustices of Soviet society as it was developing in the 20s. He does this through the medium of the visit of the devil, Woland, to Moscow, with his cat, Behemoth, and entourage. Through the havoc they cause everyone is shown up in his true colours. He juxtaposes this story with that of the Master and his unpublished novel about Pontius Pilate and Pilate's relationship with Christ, whom he must, reluctantly, condemn to death. The obvious parallels are wittily and brilliantly drawn with Stalin's Moscow ever present in the background.

Bulgakov lived in the early 1920s in a flat on the Garden Ring, No. 10, Bolshaya Sadovaya, flat 50, where he located Woland and Behemoth to carry out their shenanigans. The flat, inside a courtyard and up a flight of stairs, became a place of pilgrimage for lovers of the novel in the mid-80s to the intense irritation of those living there. A steel door was erected to keep out unwanted visitors at the top-floor entrance, but the coded courtyard door was still open to fans (who painted the new code each time it was changed on the walls outside). They gleefully and with some artistry embellished the four floors of the staircase with quotations from the novel and drawings and paintings of their favourite characters especially the sinister features of the black cat, Behemoth. Recently, the beleaguered tenants have departed and Bulgakov's old flat is to be made into a museum dedicated to him. It won't be half as much fun as the graffiti.

72. *Merab and Yury, the philosophers, flank Polina and her attractive room.*

· 72 ·

MERAB AND THE SENOKOSOVS

The Senokosovs' flat has become, in recent years, something of a political and literary salon. Yury Senokosov is a history graduate at the University of Moscow and an editor of *Questions of Philosophy*, the influential journal. He is at present involved in publishing the works of the Russian philosophers of the twentieth century, many of whom were expelled in the famous 'Ship of Philosophers' in 1922. They include the important religious thinkers, Pavel Florinsky, Lev Karsavin and Semyon Frank. Some years ago Yury was dismissed from the journal when his daughter, Tanya, went to live abroad but with the more open policy of the Soviet Union he has been able to recover his position. He and his wife, Lena, an art historian, seem to know all the most interesting people in Moscow and the great debate on the future of the Soviet Union rages constantly in their flat.

Yury's great friend and mentor was Merab Mamardashvili, the Georgian philosopher and teacher, born, ironically, in Gori the birthplace of Stalin. Merab, a moral philosopher who liked to refer to himself as a dissident philosopher, was dismissed from Moscow University in 1973, but was able to continue his work at the Academy of Sciences of Georgia in Tbilisi when Shevardnadze, the former Soviet Foreign Minister, was First Party Secretary there. His brilliance and daring, so disliked by the Conservatives, made him the centre of Georgian political and intellectual life during *glasnost*. Unfortunately he died suddenly in November 1990.

The room where the photograph was taken belongs to Polina, Lena's mother, now in her eighties. It is dominated by nineteenth-century mahogany furniture and some fine pieces of porcelain although the little piggy bank stands out, a gift from Polina's granddaughter when she was small. Even the light fitting, typical of the 50s, harmonizes well with the dark furniture. The piano is very much a part of the flat of a Moscow *intelligentsia*. This relatively large apartment was acquired by combining their previous flat with the small apartment of Yury's and exchanging them both, in time-honoured Moscow tradition, for this one large, well-located apartment.

73

YEVGENY YEVTUSHENKO

Some of the seven skyscraper 'wedding-cake' palaces built under Stalin in the 1940s and 50s which circle Moscow like a necklace are used to house apartments for favoured people. Behind one of these, the Ukraine Hotel, low wings extend back with shops on the ground floor and large, four-room apartments above. The poet Yevgeny Yevtushenko has at his disposal one such flat, though he prefers the quiet and relative seclusion of his dacha at Peredelkino, only half an hour away by car, to city living.

The apartment used to belong to a circus acrobat, first husband of Galina Brezhnev, the daughter of the former Party General Secretary and when Yevtushenko first acquired the flat he found trapeze poles fixed in the hall. One of Yevtushenko's favourite artists is Oleg Tselkov, now living in Paris, whose distorted red and black faces can be seen at the top left-hand corner of the photograph. Another is Ferdinand Leger, one of whose paintings is immediately below the light fitting on the lower right of the photograph.

Yevtushenko, a towering and controversial figure in the world of Russian literature, is sometimes known as the *shpana* or hooligan of Russian poetry. He published his first verses at the age of sixteen and a fine, narrative autobiographical poem 'Zima Station' at the age of twenty-three. He is best known for his political or 'publicistic' poems fighting causes, such as 'Stalin's Heirs' (1962) warning of a possible revival of Stalinism and, above all, his passionate attack on anti-semitism, 'Babi Yar' (1961). In 'Babi Yar' he recalls the terrible massacre of Jews and Ukrainians by the Germans at a ravine near Kiev during the last war. A monument has now been erected as a direct result of the public impact of this poem which Shostakovich incorporated in the first movement of his Thirteenth Symphony.

The late 50s and early 60s was a golden age of Soviet poetry in which Yevtushenko played a major part. Khrushchev's denunciation of Stalin in 1956 and the cultural thaw had led to an intoxicating feeling that things were about to change. But Khrushchev's attitude to the arts was not liberal and the brakes were once more applied. Before that, however, Yevtushenko and other poets like Akhmadulina (his second wife) and Voznesensky gave emotional poetry readings to tens of thousands in Mayakovsky Square, in auditoriums, sometimes even at the Lenin Stadium. They were like pop stars, the youthful audience hanging on their every word. Poetry is revered in Russia as perhaps in no other country and a popular poet is known throughout the land.

Yevtushenko, who likes to wear unconventional clothes like his famous red silk suit, has charisma, a certain audacity, which still characterizes his actions. In December 1985, when *perestroika* had only just begun, he made a remarkably outspoken speech at the Russian Writers' Congress anticipating all the major issues later aired under *glasnost*; the Stalinist purges, the brutality of collectivization, privileges of the élite, food shortages and so on. He was elected to the Congress of Peoples' Deputies in 1989 and takes an active part in organizing and participating in the demonstrations and meetings of the more radical deputies. He is also a member of the council of Memorial, the organization which aims to find out and publish information on all those who were shot or repressed in the Stalin terror of the 1930s.

Yevtushenko is a keen photographer whose work, particularly of his native Siberia, has often been exhibited. In the 1980s he started a new career making films. These include the autobiographical *Kindergarten* released in 1984 which depicted the evacuation of Moscow in 1941 and Yevtushenko's childhood experiences in wartime Siberia where paper was so scarce schoolchildren learnt to write between the lines of newspaper. Another remarkable film he made was released in 1990, *The Funeral of Stalin*, which shows the reactions of the Moscow population to the death of Stalin. Based on Yevtushenko's own experiences at the age of twenty, it graphically portrays the tragedy when huge crowds gathered spontaneously near the House of Unions in an endeavour to view Stalin's body. In the struggle the crowd inadvertently crushed to death dozens of innocent men, women and children.

73. Yevgeny Yevtushenko in his town apartment with paintings by Ferdinand Leger and Oleg Tselkov.

74A. Igumnov Mansion: the brilliant pseudo-Russian main hall and staircase.

SOUTH MOSCOW

74B. Igumnov Mansion: the doorway of the main hall.

South Moscow, in Russian, *Zamoskvoreche,* which literally translates as 'across the Moskva River', is that part of the city facing the south wall of the Kremlin from across the water. Still relatively undeveloped, its four main roads flow in a north-south direction so that the Kremlin cathedrals and palaces, clustered together on the high bank of the Moskva, constantly provide magnificent views. Not a fashionable district for the aristocracy, the population of Zamoskvoreche in the nineteenth century was made up of more ordinary people – merchants, priests, civil servants. Small factories began to appear in some numbers changing the face of the area by the end of the century, but not completely obliterating its quiet, residential air rent with the peals of bells from the numerous churches. Its streets today are still lined with small, late classical houses interspersed with tall churches and the eccentric mansions of nouveau-riche merchants. Alexander Ostrovsky, the outstanding pre-Revolutionary playwright, was born here and Pavel Tretyakov, of a merchant family, founded his great gallery of Russian art here in his own home which has recently been comprehensively reconstructed and extended.

Immediately in front of the Kremlin is the narrow island created by the 1786 drainage canal where, in the sixteenth and seventeenth centuries, the Tsars' extensive market gardens provided food for the large population of the Kremlin. The island contains the forbidding Government House built in 1928 to provide apartments for influential members of the Party and Government. So many people were arrested in the 30s from this apartment block that one of its walls can barely contain all the plaques commemorating those since rehabilitated. A hundred yards further down the embankment outside the mansion facing the Great Kremlin Palace across the river, the Union Jack flies bravely – the British Embassy has the most enviable position of all foreign missions in Moscow.

Dimitrov Street is the furthest west of the main north-south routes and, in recent years, has been subjected the most to monotonous redevelopment. However, the colourful, romantic form of the neo-Russian Igumnov Mansion, now the French Embassy, on one side and the red and white tower of the Church of St John the Warrior on the other, save it from banality.

The parallel road, Bolshaya Polyanka, is more satisfying. Here, the Church of St Gregory with its liberal use of coloured tiles makes a vivid contrast to the old yellowing houses which line the curved street. Between Bolshaya Polyanka and the next main road, Bolshaya Ordynka, are many charming lanes on one of which the magnificent Tretyakov Gallery is located.

Bolshaya Ordynka is the quietest of the main streets featuring beautiful churches, some on nearby lanes like the breathtaking Sts Michael and Fyodor, and the tall, elegant Church of the Resurrection in Kadashy. Moscow's important medieval settlement of weavers, the Kadashy, was found in this part of Moscow conveniently close to the Court. Other medieval settlements included the Royal coiners, musketeers, sheepskin tanners and smiths. There are five more churches on Bolshaya Ordynka itself including the Consolation of All Sorrows, one of the finest examples of late classicism in church architecture. Another most unusual church is the charming Art Nouveau Church of the Intercession designed for the Martha-Mary Community in 1911 by Aleksei Shchusev.

The last radial street, Pyatnitskaya, is named after the church demolished in the 1930s to build the Novokuznetskaya Metro Station, famous for its sculptures. Pyatnitskaya, the busiest street of Zamoskvoreche, has retained its old shops including a turn-of-the-century confectioner. The street's gently curving line is given vertical definition at one end by the tall bell-tower of St John and at the other by the soaring baroque Church of St Clement.

Beyond the Garden Ring, which encloses the old part of Zamoskvoreche, new Moscow begins. Here there were no inhibitions to prevent large-scale redevelopment and much of the older housing has been levelled and rebuilt. The splendid

Donskoi Monastery, however, remains unscathed. Some of the most interesting communal housing developments of the 1920s took place here, including the fine constructivist students' block by Nikolaev on Ordzhonikidze Street.

The broad Leninsky Prospekt runs south from Dimitrov Street and leads ultimately to Vnukovo Airport. In the eighteenth- and nineteenth-centuries mansions and palaces of influential princes and counts were built on the left side of the road with wide gardens descending to the river (now incorporated into Gorky Park). The finest of these palaces was the Alexandra or Neskuchny Sad, built under Nicholas I, now used by the Academy of Sciences. Almost next door are three old hospitals backing onto Gorky Park. The oldest one, founded in 1800 by Prince Golitsyn, is reckoned to be the masterpiece of the leading classical architect, Matvei Kazakov. Across Leninsky Prospekt are more charity hospitals erected in the early years of the twentieth century by means of private donations. All these hospitals are still in use.

Further out, where the river makes a wide loop, the land rises to a high plateau. In a leafy ravine are the laboratories and workshops of the Academy of Sciences' physics institutes, including the splendid Italianate villa that was used by the Nobel Prize winner, Peter Kapitsa. Further on the huge new University of Moscow building, monumental and impressive, the best of the Stalin wedding-cake palaces, stands on the plateau overlooking Moscow.

The area south of the university is known as *Yugozapad* or South-west. Because the university and Academy of Sciences institutes are located in this district thereby attracting university lecturers and scientists, it has become one of the more desirable of the new residential areas of Moscow. Grouped together to one side of the university are three popular children's institutions; the new circus, the Pioneer Palace and the Children's Musical Theatre.

A little to the east of the university is one of the first areas to be built up in the hasty attempt to solve the overcrowding in Moscow in the late 1950s and early 60s. Dima Krasnopevtsev, the artist, and his wife Lilya live in a tiny two-room flat in one of these five-storey blocks which, although shabby and inconvenient, are less objectionable than the later high-rise towers that now dominate Moscow's skyline in every direction.

Beyond the Automobile Ring Road lie the dormitory towns which include the writers' village of Peredelkino where Pasternak is buried and where the journalist Victor Louis and his wife Jennifer live in their comfortable house with all mod-cons and the most fabulous collection of furniture from the late nineteenth and early twentieth centuries.

Reminders that the vast areas now incorporated into the city of Moscow were once villages are found in the few old churches and manor houses isolated in the sea of tower blocks. Two former royal estates are found in the southern extremities of Moscow; Kolomenskoe with its ancient, uniquely beautiful, pyramid tower church built four centuries ago and the red and white 200-year-old ruins of Tsaritsyno, Empress Catherine's folly, abandoned when almost complete.

Times are changing. On a hill almost at the edge of Moscow and surrounded by the ubiquitous towers a new Russian Orthodox Church is being erected, the first to be built in Moscow since the Revolution.

74C. Igumnov Mansion: a detail of the remarkable plasterwork of the salon.

74D. Igumnov Mansion: the first-floor salon with original tapestries and chandelier.

74

THE IGUMNOV MANSION
(THE FRENCH EMBASSY)

Dimitrov Street forms part of the route along which state visitors arriving at Vnukovo Airport are conveyed to the Kremlin. As they draw near the centre where this rather dull avenue meets the Garden Ring Road, they cannot fail to notice a curious mansion with sloping roofs, balconies, pendules, coloured tiles, arches and peaked roof porches, a crazy patchwork of motifs and themes from Russian wooden medieval architecture. The architect, Nikolai Pozdeyev from Yaroslavl, itself an ancient city that could well illustrate a Russian fairy-tale, was obviously inspired by the slavophiles and the neo-Russian style. His genius lay in the ability to amalgamate such disparate stylistic elements into a coherent whole. When completed in 1893 for the Igumnov family, also from Yaroslavl, his mansion became something of a *cause célèbre*, attacked by many as too wedded to archaic motifs. But the leading art historian of the day, Valery Stasov, declared in its favour and it inspired the young Aleksei Shchusev, future designer of the Kazan Railway Station and the Lenin Mausoleum, to make architecture his career. Sadly, Pozdeyev died in the very year of the completion of the unique house, his masterpiece, not by hanging himself in the front hall as legend has it, but of tuberculosis.

The interior is as astonishing as the exterior. The main hall and staircase in particular abound in every conceivable

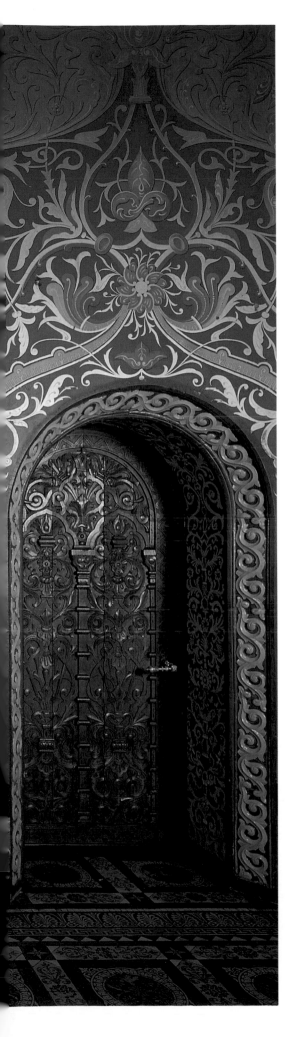

74. *Igumnov Mansion: E: the doors of the main hall resemble those of the Kremlin Terem Palace.*
F: the dining-room inspired by medieval architecture.

decoration – chevrons, beaded work and metalwork in lovely tulip designs. Repeated everywhere is the fleur de lys in the tiles of the floor and in the painted walls. The stairs of grey and white marble lead past walls in multicoloured designs relieved only slightly by large areas of light grey. Even the vaulted ceilings do not interrupt the design. There is a feeling in the hall and staircase of a medieval 'palata' where not symmetry but colour and comfort are the main passion of the builder.

The reception rooms are totally different. The main salon is decorated with ornate baroque mouldings and a heavy chandelier. Above the cornices, heavy-breasted women play the lyre or hold palette and brush supporting medallions of what seem to be portraits of leading Russians – Pushkin's is easily identifiable. Only the dining-room continues the medieval theme with vaulted ceilings and heavy wooden doors.

After the Revolution the house became a medical institute and then a workers' club. In 1938 it was handed over to the French government as its embassy. With the building of a new office block next door, the French are able to use the mansion solely as the residence of their ambassador.

· 75 ·

DIMA AND LILYA
KRASNOPEVTSEV

The southern suburbs of Moscow were the object of intensive building activity in the late 1950s when Khrushchev, in typically grandiose manner, attempted to solve the shameful overcrowding of the heavily congested centre. Thousands of five-storey blocks of flats were erected in a landscape bare and uninviting at the time, far from the amenities of the town and shorn of the old villages by the omnipresent bulldozers. Nevertheless, residents of central Moscow, where a family per room was the norm and forty people could be sharing a toilet and cooking facilities, were often grateful for the small, but self-contained apartments in the new, hastily erected blocks.

The flats were contemptuously known as *Khrushchoby*, a play on the words Khrushchev and *trushchoby* (slums), although with the maturing of the trees around them, they now fit more happily into the landscape. Shops and transport have gradually improved over the years and the flats no longer seem to be in the back of beyond as new Moscow has grown far beyond them. Dima Krasnopevtsev, the artist, and his wife Lilya, the art historian and television producer, live in one of the *Khrushchoby* flats to which they moved over twenty years ago from the attractive district of Ostozhenka in the centre of Moscow.

Dima was a gifted student of the Surikov Art Institute in the late 40s. His style has not greatly altered over his working life; he paints slowly and precisely in subdued hues still lifes, classical vases, branches and bottles, which seem to have within them their own, sometimes disturbing personalities. As his paintings suggest, he is an intellectual and an avid francophile. His studio is carefully hung with beautiful natural objects; rare stones, curious shells, bones, fossils, some sent to him from all over the world. Icons line the walls and he has a charming collection of miniature Roman bottles. Bunches of large, medieval keys hang over the doorway.

Dima, always supported and encouraged by his wife, Lilya, has had to struggle for many decades unrecognized, unable to take part in exhibitions or gain membership of the Union of Artists and enjoy its patronage. In his late fifties, he finally became a member of the union, but has remained aloof from the art establishment of the Soviet Union. He is now recognized as one of the most interesting of the Soviet artists to have come out of the underground of the last forty years. In 1988 Sotheby's included several of his paintings in their successful Moscow sale and much of his work has now found its way abroad. Even the Pushkin Gallery has purchased Krasnopevtsevs for its collection.

75A. The Krasnopevtsevs: Dima in his studio surrounded by the rare objects that inspire his paintings.

75B. The Kranopevtsevs: Lilya with Dima's paintings behind her.

A

THE KHARITONENKO
MANSION
(THE BRITISH EMBASSY)

The grand mansion, built for the Kharitonenko family in 1891 by the architect, B.G. Zalessky, on the south embankment of the Moskva River, is in an ideal position. The house is set back from the street behind iron fencing facing the river where, on the opposite bank, the Kremlin cathedrals and churches with their thirty golden domes and the great Kremlin Palace provide an incomparable backdrop.

As in so many grand houses of this era in Moscow, the Kharitonenko Mansion is the work of the most imaginative and versatile architect of the time, Fyodor Shekhtel. Inside, all is heavy, dark, oak panelling, with linenfolds and pointed arches, a neo-Gothic gloom. Immediately the heavy staircase with newel posts like tall hats leads upwards. The Gothic impression is sustained in the darkly panelled hall upstairs with grand fireplace and heavy fire-irons and two exquisite original tapestries on the walls. But here the reception rooms begin to differ in style one from the other. The Blue Room (now finished in beige) features mischievous elves hanging on the lintels of the doors and a heavily carved

B

76. Kharitonenko Mansion: A: the main staircase and upper hall with original tapestries. B: an elf over the doorway of the Blue Room.

fireplace. Next door, the Red Room displays a different style, that of Francois I, the sixteenth-century King of France; his salamander and porcupine are depicted on the fireplace. A balcony provides magnificent views of the Kremlin.

Next is the ballroom, all in white and gold, even to the furniture, some of which is original. Only the patterns of the intricate parquet flooring and the original painting on the wall vary the overall design. Then comes the dining-room, originally the picture gallery, dark and heavy with a splendid painting of musicians and promenaders on the ceiling and, on the walls, large portraits of the British Kings and Queens from a youthful Queen Victoria to George V. For the mansion is, and has been for the past sixty years, the British Embassy where Churchill and Stalin and many other heads of state and prime ministers have been entertained.

When the Kharitonenkos, famous for their musical evenings where Scriabin and

76C. Kharitonenko Mansion: the dining-room with portrait of Edward VII.

76B. Kharitonenko Mansion: the dining-room ceiling painting by Francois Flameng.

76E. Kharitonenko Mansion: a view of the Kremlin from the Red Room.

76F. Kharitonenko Mansion: the carved wooden fireplace of the Blue Room.

Chaliapin performed, left after the Revolution, the house was taken over by the new Soviet Foreign Ministry as a guest house. Such diverse persons as H.G. Wells, Enver Pasha and the King and Queen of Afghanistan enjoyed the government hospitality. The Soviet Commissar for Foreign Affairs, Maxim Litvinov, and his English wife also had an apartment there. In 1930 it became the British Embassy since when many successive generations of diplomats have enjoyed its matchless view of the Kremlin. Among notable dinners was the one given for Churchill and Stalin in 1944.

H

76. Kharitonenko Mansion: G: the white and gold ballroom with a portrait of the Queen. H: looking from the white and gold room into the dining-room.

77A. St John the Warrior: the wooden iconostasis of the early eighteenth century.

· 77 ·

THE CHURCH OF ST JOHN
THE WARRIOR

According to tradition the site for St John was chosen by Peter the Great during the Great Flood of 1709 when he noticed a church inundated by the flood waters. On learning it was dedicated to the warrior saint whom he admired he declared that a new church of the same name should be erected on the highest place on the street and that he himself would provide the plan. This he did, appointing the experienced architect, artist and sculptor from the Ukraine, Ivan Zarudny, to oversee the work. Zarudny was the designer of the Church of the Archangel Gabriel in Moscow and of the impressive guilt iconostasis

in the Cathedral of Sts Peter and Paul in St Petersberg (Leningrad). In 1707 Zarudny had been appointed the Tsar's supervisor of painting, both religious and secular, in Russia with the title of 'Superintendant'. The Church of St John was also built to honour the great Russian victory against the Swedish army at Poltava in 1709, the turning-point in Peter's long struggle against Charles XII of Sweden. Zarudny had built a florid triumphal arch in Red Square in honour of the return of Peter the Great's victorious troops after the battle.

St John was completed in 1713, just before the Tsar banned further building in Moscow in order to concentrate on the construction of his new capital, St Petersburg. This is one of the few buildings erected in Moscow under Peter the Great and at the same time one of the last to be completed before the slump in Moscow's fortunes in favour of the new capital which lasted until

the end of the eighteenth century.

Architecturally, too, St John plays an important role, bridging the gap between the purely Moscow form of baroque and the western style which began to appear at the beginning of the eighteenth century. Within, its open octagonal receding tower soars above the central part of the church betraying its Moscow origins but revealing western European influence in the prolific use of sculptured mouldings. The interior arrangement of the church, however, is strictly traditional — refectory (ante-room) followed by the main part of the church, with, on the east wall, the iconostasis closing off the apse. Vasily Bazhenov, the leading architect of the Empress Catherine, was a great admirer of St John and adapted its tower form to his neo-Gothic palaces.

In the religious history of Moscow, St John occupies a special place. Almost unique in the Soviet period, St John, even during the godless 1930s, was never closed. Most churches that were not demolished (some 240 in Moscow alone were destroyed), were forcibly closed for a time and then reopened during the period of improved relations with the Church in the Second World War. Priests and parishioners looked on St John as a haven for the valuable icons and relics of the closed and demolished churches. Thus the church harbours many treasures, including an old icon of St Basil from the famous cathedral in Red Square, the icon of the Saviour which hung over the Kremlin

Saviour Gate (on the right in the photograph), the wonderfully carved wooden iconostasis from the seventeenth-century Church of the Resurrection in Kadashy, and over 150 relics of saints.

St John draws its congregation from afar, as for a long time there were few other working churches in the south-west part of Moscow beyond the Garden Ring. Since 1988 two others have reopened and a new church is to be built, relieving the pressure on St John and helping the elderly, who have had to travel long distances, to attend services.

77B. St John the Warrior: a view of the inner side of the octagonal tower.

THE CHURCH OF THE CONSOLATION OF ALL SORROWS

The Church of the Consolation of All Sorrows, one of the best classical buildings in Moscow, is named after the important icon, a copy of which was made for Peter the Great's sister, who took it to the new capital, St Petersburg. Built in the shape of a rotunda, its architecture is most interesting, for it combines the early strict classical period of the 1780s with the post-1812, more decorative Russian Empire. It also embodies the work of two of the most notable architects of those periods, Vasily Bazhenov and Osip Bove.

Bazhenov, court architect to Catherine II until he fell from favour, was commissioned in 1783 to rebuild the older seventeenth-century church; he added a new narthex and a round tiered bell-tower.

When the reconstructed church was damaged by fire in 1812 it was decided to rebuild the sanctuary as well. This Bove did in 1828-33 in the form of a rotunda defined by a colonnade which blends exceptionally well with Bazhenov's conception.

Inside, the effect is palatial and, to Russian eyes used to the narrow, heavily painted interiors of older churches, somewhat secular. Oil paintings rather than wall frescoes predominate, giving it more the air of an Italian than a Russian Church. Bazhenov's narthex with its columns leads towards Bove's sanctuary, all gold and blue and white, the circular area defined by Ionic columns which support a frieze and the dome itself. The unusual circular floor is made of decorative iron slabs from the Demidov metalworks in the Urals and is contemporary with the building. The classical iconostasis, with fewer tiers than usual, is somewhat overwhelmed by the columns and friezes of the architecture and does not command attention in the same way as iconostases in more traditional churches.

One of the few functioning churches in Moscow before the era of Gorbachev's reforms (it was closed 1938-47), it was famous for the performance of Rachmaninov's Vespers on the anniversary of his birth which was, until recently (like other

B

78. *Consolation of All Sorrows: A: the inner side of the circular dome.*
B: the classical iconostasis and iron floor.

religious music), never performed in the concert halls of Moscow. Orthodox churches do not allow musical instruments, preferring the natural tones of the human voice, and singing forms an integral part of every service.

The popular parish priest, Father Boris, has recently entered the political fray that has overtaken Moscow with the advent of free elections. He and several of his colleagues from other churches were elected to the local council, the Zamoskvoreche Soviet. This seems astonishing in view of the restricted role priests have been allowed to play since the Revolution; for a long time they were even denied their civic rights.

· 79 ·

THE CHILDREN'S MUSICAL THEATRE

In the south part of Moscow near the new university are three impressive buildings, one after the other, all devoted to the amusement and education of children: the 'new' circus built in 1971; the Pioneers' Palace opened in the early sixties; and, the latest and most innovative, the Children's Musical Theatre.

The entire concept of the theatre is due to the energy and vision of one remarkable

79. *Children's Musical Theatre: A: the Palekh music room. B: the rotunda with filigree bird-cage.*

person, Natalya Sats, now in her late eighties but still indomitable. She is the daughter of the composer, Ilya Sats, who was musical director and composer for the Moscow Arts Theatre under Stanislavsky. Natalya, too, was smitten by the theatre and after the Revolution, when still in her teens, set up the Central Children's Theatre. She was passionately interested in combining music with drama and her great enthusiasm inspired the composer, Sergei Prokofiev, to write the words and music of his famous fairy-tale *Peter and the Wolf* in 1936.

Tragedy struck in 1937 when her husband, Marshall Tukhachevsky, the leading figure in the Soviet Army, was arrested and executed. Shortly afterwards she, too, was arrested and sent to a camp in Siberia where she spent sixteen years, freed only after Stalin's death in 1953. She was then able to return to the Children's Theatre and to continue her career; Marshall Tukhachevsky was finally rehabilitated in 1958.

In 1965 her struggle to establish a sepa-

rate Children's Musical Theatre was finally successful and it set up shop in a tiny hall. After further strenuous agitation Natalya Sats was able to persuade the authorities to build a new, purpose-built theatre in south-west Moscow. The theatre opened in 1980, appropriately the Year of the Child, its design far superior to most modern buildings then being erected in Moscow. It is composed of a long wall above which rise three cylinders of different heights; the central one, on which stands a bluebird, the emblem of happiness, encloses the stage for the main auditorium.

The interior has been charmingly designed to incorporate the Palekh room with its great panels painted in the form of lacquer boxes illustrating various tales and the airy and delicate bird-cage rotunda. Before each play the adult actors in their elaborate costumes — bears, roosters, lions — come out to the foyer to talk to the children enhancing the fairy-tale atmosphere of the theatre.

80A. Neskuchny Sad: the wrought iron and brass staircase by Bove.

80B. Neskuchny Sad: a detail of a ceiling in one of the garden-facing rooms.

· 80 ·

NESKUCHNY SAD
(THE ALEXANDRA PALACE)

Neskuchny Sad (Pleasaunce Garden) or the Alexandra Palace, named after the wife of Nicholas I, had a long history of different landlords before it became one of the few royal residences in Moscow. Under its present owners, the Academy of Sciences, it has survived the period since the Revolution well. Here in palatial surroundings overlooking the lovely garden are the offices of Academician Marchuk, the President of the Academy, and Academician Velikhov, the Vice-President, and adviser on scientific affairs to Gorbachev.

Nicholas I purchased the property after his coronation in 1826 from three estates; from the Trubetskoi family who owned Neskuchny Gardens, from the Demidov and Orlov families who built the original palace, and, in 1842, from the Golitsyn estate which the formidable old Princess in her nineties, the model for Pushkin's old Countess in *Queen of Spades*, had refused to sell even to the Tsar himself while she was alive.

The mansion was first built in 1756 by the Demidov family, the great entrepreneurs of mining in the Urals, who loved to arrange lavish entertainments. The house was designed by architect Yest in the form of a square block, its façade facing the river. An oval courtyard flanked by Corinthian columns greeted visitors entering the house. In the 1790s under Count Orlov-Chesmensky, the confederate of Catherine II when she seized the throne from Peter III, the house was considerably altered with its ceremonial entrance moved to the back.

After its purchase by the Tsar the court architect, Yevgraf Tyurin, added further embellishments in the form of attractive

80C. Neskuchny Sad: a detail of the ceiling of the oval room.

semicircular balconies on either side of the front portico. The elegant rooms on the first floor are among the finest examples in Moscow of the Empire style with columns in polished artificial marble and ceilings with fine mouldings and superb paintings. The unusual wrought-iron and brass staircase was the work of Osip Bove, the city architect, in 1834.

In the late nineteenth century Grand Duke Sergey, the uncle of Nicholas II and Governor-General of Moscow, was granted tenancy of the palace and the right of Muscovites to enjoy the gardens then ceased. After the Revolution the palace was nationalized. Over four hundred pieces of furniture, vases and paintings originally in the palace are still in situ.

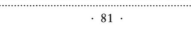

· 81 ·

VICTOR AND JENNIFER LOUIS

Victor Louis, a Russian in spite of his name, is one of the most enigmatic people in Moscow. He is a journalist who writes for western newspapers, and is married to Jennifer, his English wife. He served nine years in the prison camps of the *gulag* in the late 1940s and 50s. He is now one of the most wealthy people in Moscow, with a house and garden at Peredelkino, exotic furniture and a garage full of vintage cars, that would not look out of place in the stockbroker belt of the Home Counties in England or on the eastern seaboard of the

United States. In Moscow his lifestyle is simply extraordinary and few journalists could emulate it.

Victor is justifiably proud of how he has furnished his house. So many people in the 60s and 70s were moved from large old flats in the centre to the smaller, but self-contained, apartments in the tower blocks, that he was able to pick up beautiful but cumbersome old pieces for very little. Some rooms are decorated with exquisite pieces of Art Nouveau, and others are in the neo-Russian style harking back to Russian traditional furniture that was popular around 1900.

The Louis are seated in their study furnished with magnificent, heavy Italian furniture which, although acquired at

81. Victor and Jennifer Louis in the study of their country house.

different times, all fits together comfortably. The reclining chair on which Victor is sitting is really a Russian sleigh with runners and armrests of curving swan necks. At the back of the study is Victor's collection of sixty-four small busts of notable Russians — aristocrats and famous men — picked up in odd places as far away as New York.

Victor, once known as the mouthpiece of the Kremlin, was for a long time correspondent for various English newspapers and, in his time, obtained many amazing stories through his incomparable connections. Perhaps his most famous scoop was the report that Khrushchev had been removed from power in October 1964, which appeared in the pages of the *Evening News* hours before it was officially announced. His ambivalent role in purveying to the West pirated manuscripts of Solzhenitsyn's *Cancer Ward*, Svetlana Stalin's memoirs and photographs of Academician Sakharov during his exile in Gorky earned him considerable notoriety. *Glasnost* has limited his exclusivity.

His wife, Jennifer, annually produces the invaluable *Information Moscow*, a directory of foreign embassies and businesses in Moscow and, with Victor, she also writes guide books. Her main passion, however, is the cultivated garden, something virtually unknown in Moscow, but which she has somehow created in inhospitable surroundings. Jennifer remains at the core deeply English, a stalwart of the Anglican community in Moscow and on Christmas Day she will always be found listening to the Queen's Speech.

· 82 ·

THE NEW UNIVERSITY

After the Second World War the Soviet Union faced the immense problem of restoring its economy and devastated cities in the formerly occupied areas. It was decided in 1947, at Stalin's behest, to embark on an enormously costly plan to embellish the capital by building eight skyscrapers in salient positions around the centre of Moscow. They were to be grouped around a gigantic Palace of Soviets, which, surmounted by a large statue of Lenin, was to be taller than the Empire State Building. The construction problems of the Palace of Soviets fortu-

nately proved too difficult to overcome and the project was eventually abandoned. However, all but one of the high-rise towers, popularly known as Stalin's wedding-cake palaces, were built. Grotesque they undoubtedly are, but also oddly successful in providing vertical points of interest like the Gothic cathedrals of western Europe.

Designed by a team of architects led by the talented Lev Rudnev, the university buildings in the Lenin Hills overlooking the Moskva River are the largest and tallest of the skyscrapers. The central part rises thirty-six stories high and is flanked by four huge 'wings' on each corner, which are linked to the central block. In the course of building it was decided to accentuate further the vertical line by adding a tall spire.

The old university housed in a superb classical mansion in the centre, contains the journalism, psychology and law faculties. Out at the Lenin Hills a new concept of a university campus developed. The huge building with its extended wings is really an entirely self-contained town with a population of over 30,000 including, among the genuine students, a large, illegal population which the authorities try in vain to control. As a result a pass is always needed to enter and leave the building.

On the ground floor there are two open foyers with colonnades lined with medallions of leading world scientists and with figures in bronze of major Soviet scientists at each end. Like some of the metro stations, these halls are the epitome of sombre Soviet classicism and it is perhaps significant that students are rarely encountered in these serene, magisterial places. In the photograph the seated figure at the end of the hall against a marble wall is Ivan Michurin (1855-1935), the biologist who created a number of special varieties of fruit trees suitable for the cold Russian climate through skilful crossing. However, he also introduced to Soviet science the theory of the inheritance of acquired characteristics which inspired the spurious ideas of Lysenko, who tyrannized genuine Soviet biologists and geneticists in the Stalin period. A quote by Michurin is displayed on the wall 'We cannot await charity from nature. To take it from nature is our task . . .'

82. New University: a formal foyer of one of the 1953 skyscrapers.

· 83 ·

THE PALACE OF YOUTH

The idea of palaces for the people is an inherently Soviet one. After the Revolution, in the first flush of enthusiasm, the new communist state determined to demonstrate its intention to redress the balance in living conditions between the well-off and the mass of the population by building grandiose public buildings, palaces for all. Competitions were held for the gigantic Palace of Labour (never built), the Palace of Industry (never built) and the even larger Palace of Soviets (started but never completed). On a less ambitious scale, many Palaces of Culture were built and eventually, the Palace of Congresses (1961), the Palace of Pioneers (1962) and, in 1987, the Palace of Youth were constructed. 'Palace' meant a large, public building in the massive neo-classical style which the communist regime had always automatically associated with power and wealth.

Prospekt may well be the last in this tradition of Soviet palaces. Commissioned some years ago by the Komsomol organization (Youth Group of the Communist Party), it took a long time to build and, when completed in 1987, already seemed dated and out of place. It was built on the broad Komsomol Avenue in front of old gardens with the early nineteenth-century Khamovnichesky Barracks on one side. Large and pompous in the shape of a white box with giant pylon-like columns supporting the roof along two façades, it does not fit comfortably into its historical site. Inside are two halls, one large and one small, with a deep enclosed courtyard between them. The small hall, with a bust of Lenin at one end, has a reverential atmosphere rather like a chapel. The chief architect was the egregious Mikhail Posokhin, city architect for twenty-two years and involved in nearly every major new building in Moscow in that time.

One of the first exhibitions to be held at the Palace of Youth was of the work of the enormously popular artist, Ilya Glazunov, whose paintings on historical subjects have a strong religious and Russian nationalist flavour. Six months later the extraordinary Labyrinth exhibition opened with art of all genres and styles by artists previously unshown and unknown. Another exhibition

83. Palace of Youth: the bust of Lenin stands in the centre of the hall.

which shook Moscow was one of the Khrushchev period, Those Ten Years, in the summer of 1989. Organized by the Khrushchev family, making liberal use of family archives, it was no whitewash of the Khrushchev era, but an objective portrayal of the events and atmosphere of the years in which Khrushchev was in power, beginning with his ascent in the 30s, and finishing with his fall in 1964. It recalled not only Khrushchev's anti-Stalin campaign and the release and rehabilitation of political prisoners, but his brow-beating of writers, artists and his persecution of the Church. One of the exhibits, a mock-up of a kitchen in a communal flat, illustrated in the grandiose Palace of Youth the contrast in the Soviet state between public splendour and private squalor.

· 84 ·

ANNA KAPITSA

Moscow is full of surprising nooks and crannies. Out in the Lenin Hills overlooking the Moskva River and the Andreyev Monastery is a large estate which includes an eighteenth-century house, now the property of the Academy of Sciences. Tucked away at the back amid trees and a gurgling stream is one of the most charming houses in Moscow.

It was built in the 1930s by the architect Yevgeny Stamo and is a small Italianate villa with a rusticated façade fitting beautifully into the country setting. The villa was

given to the outstanding scientist and physicist, Peter Kapitsa, member of the Royal Academy and winner of the 1978 Nobel Prize for Physics. He established the laboratory for his Institute of Problems of Physics (magnetic fields and high temperatures) in this idyllic setting and also lived here with his wife and two sons.

Peter Kapitsa, who died in 1984, had an extraordinarily eventful and arduous life. As a young physicist in Petrograd working in the laboratory of his teacher, Adam Joffe, he suffered a terrible tragedy when he lost his father, wife and baby daughter in the terrible winter of 1919-20. In 1921 Joffe made arrangements for the despairing young man to join a delegation of the new Soviet Academy of Sciences on a trip to England. He met Ernest Rutherford in

84. Anna Kapitsa in the sitting-room of the Italianate villa.

Cambridge who immediately invited the young Russian scientist to join him at the Cavendish Laboratories. Kapitsa was to work there for thirteen years, and to achieve such outstanding success that his own laboratory was especially built for him and opened in 1933.

Kapitsa, at the height of his career and married to a Russian *émigrée*, Anna Krylova, visited Leningrad in 1934 to see his mother. However, Stalin prevented him from returning to Cambridge. After a year Anna, with their sons, travelled to the country she had escaped from as a young girl and the family was reunited. Stalin had promised Kapitsa all possible facilities, but he needed vital equipment left behind in Cambridge. Lord Rutherford generously shipped it to Moscow where Kapitsa was allowed to set up his new institute.

Here his troubles did not end, for by the late 1930s Stalin's reign of terror was in full swing. When the brilliant young physicist, Lev Landau (later recipient of the Nobel Prize), was arrested in 1938, Kapitsa immediately wrote to Stalin. However, it was a year before Landau was freed and only on the understanding that Kapitsa would be personally responsible for him. Kapitsa himself suffered harassment, particularly after refusing to work on the atomic bomb. Under house arrest for a decade, he was only able to live a normal life again in 1955 and travel abroad, revisiting his beloved Cambridge. In 1978 in Stockholm he received the Nobel Prize. In 1989 Kapitsa's remarkable correspondence with the Soviet leadership was published. Among the correspondents were Beria, Stalin's dread policeman, Zhdanov, responsible for strangling the arts, and Stalin himself.

The villa in the Lenin Hills continues to house a working laboratory on the ground floor. Upstairs a museum to Kapitsa has been set up where beautiful old pieces of apparatus, many of which he made himself, are on display together with many fascinating photographs. In the sitting-room is a strange collection of models of crocodiles of all sizes and materials, reminders of Ernest Rutherford, the great teacher and father of nuclear physics, who was affectionately known as 'the Crocodile'.

85. Confectionery Shop on Pyatnitskaya: the fin-de-siècle *interior is little changed.*

· 85 ·

THE CONFECTIONERY SHOP, 9 PYATNITSKAYA

Pyatnitskaya, one of the north-south main streets of Zamoskvoreche, leads towards Red Square across the Drainage Canal and the Moskva River offering occasional fine views of the grandeur of the Kremlin. Pyatnitskaya itself is an attractive street; two churches, a tall bell-tower and many late eighteenth- and early nineteenth-century houses line its route, together with the occasional early twentieth-century mansion; modern architecture rarely intrudes. It is still a street of small, useful shops, as it was before the Revolution. Judging by the constant crowds, it is highly prized by the local population.

One of the busy shops is Confectionery No. 780 located at No. 9 Pyatnitskaya. It is housed on the ground floor of a typical building of the early twentieth century. The original owner, the merchant, Mikhail Babanin, furnished the shop with attractive birchwood counters and cupboards, added the columns and moulded ceiling frieze, and opened the shop for the sale of cakes, biscuits and confectionery. Surprisingly, the shop fittings which survive almost intact include the brass rails and bronze wall light-fittings. Still a confectioner's shop, the choice of goods these days is rather narrow but tea, biscuits and one kind of cake can still be found there together with many kinds of sweets.

The jolly proprietor of the shop, Zoya, with her colleagues, after long bargaining with the Moscow City Council, has succeeded in purchasing the premises. After a short period of closing down to effect the necessary changes, it is to be reopened as a co-operative (euphemism for privately owned) confectionery cum café. They are converting the first floor into an area with tables and chairs where tea and coffee and ice-cream are served. In the summer the garden, too, will become a small café. It is an encouraging example of individual initiative made possible by the new economic reforms, but it will face problems since the tax on co-operatives has risen to 50 per cent of profits. With the election of a radical new Moscow City Council, however, small enterprises like this one stand a better chance of success.

86. Metro Novokuznetskaya: the 1943 hall shows a ceiling mosaic depicting fruit picking.

· 86 ·

METRO NOVOKUZNETSKAYA

The busy metro station Novokuznetskaya is entered by a great circular building through which people stream in and out all day. The location of the station between the streets of Pyatnitskaya and Novokuznetskaya is squarely on the site of the former Church of Paraskeva Pyatnitskaya after which the street was named. The church, a tall, tiered building of 1739 built by Moscow merchants, was demolished in the early 1930s.

Novokuznetskaya belongs to the second stage of the metro system, the Gorkovsko-Zamoskvoretskaya Line, part of which had opened in 1938. Even at the outbreak of war work continued on the line, and three stations – Novokuznetskaya, Paveletskaya and Avtozavodskaya – were completed and officially opened in 1943. The stations on this line, therefore, have a military theme.

Novokuznetskaya was designed by the architects Vladimir Gelfreikh and Igor Rozhin, who together built several other metro stations. The hall of Novokuznetskaya is decorated in light-coloured marbles interspersed with granite and, above the cornice, a frieze of bas-reliefs which depict Russian military leaders of the past: Suvorov, Minin, Pozharsky and Kutuzov, the great general of the battle against Napoleon. Among the sculptors was Nikolai Tomsky, six times winner of the State Prize, who was responsible for a great number of the major statues put up in the Soviet period in Moscow, including the absurdly cheerful figure of Gogol on the Boulevard.

The decorated ceiling is enlivened by mosaic panels in smalt (the cobalt-coloured glass often used in metro station mosaics). The panels, depicting the banal optimism of the period – girls with wreaths, athletes parading – were made by the artist, V. Frolov, in war-torn Leningrad, to the designs of Alexander Deineka. He was one of the major artists of Soviet monumental art who also designed the panels in the Mayakovskaya Metro Station. Frolov died in the siege of Leningrad but, because the construction of the metro had such high priority, the panels were brought out in boats over Lake Ladoga, the only corridor available during the siege.

87. *Golitsyn Hospital: the chapel rotunda with Ionic and Corinthian columns*

· 87 ·

THE GOLITSYN HOSPITAL

In the second half of the eighteenth century it became fashionable for wealthy members of the aristocracy to found large public institutions. Prince Dmitry Mikhailovich Golitsyn, for thirty years Russian Ambassador in Vienna, left his fortune in 1793 to the founding of a hospital for the poor in Moscow. According to his will the income from two estates (with over 2,000 'souls') and the proceeds from the sale of his remarkable collection of paintings were to fund a large new hospital 'for the sick and suffering'. The hospital was duly built in 1796-1801 in the south of Moscow on a fashionable avenue of palaces belonging to the nobility. The architect chosen by the benefactor's brother was the outstanding classical architect, Matvei Kazakov.

The Golitsyn Hospital is considered to be Kazakov's masterpiece. Three storeys high and set well back from what is now a wide highway behind a screen of trees, it is palatial in concept with a large hemispherical dome over the chapel. The building spreads horizontally, sweeping out each side with long curving wings as if protecting the central portico.

Under the dome is the spacious circular Chapel of the 'Holy Orthodox Tsarevich Prince Dmitry', two floors high and dedicated to the nine-year-old murdered son of Ivan the Terrible. It is distinguished by its harmonious colour combination with free-standing pink Ionic columns of artificial marble. Beyond these is a wall of slim grey Corinthian columns on which the wide dome with its coffered and painted inner side rests. The wall niches are filled with grisaille paintings and sculptures, one of which is of Prince Dmitry Mikhailovich himself.

The hospital, which originally contained 100 beds, is much larger today and incorporates two neighbouring institutions into one enormous First City Hospital. The Golitsyn buildings are used as a diagnostic centre specializing in eye diseases. The chapel has not functioned as a church since the Revolution and is used as a concourse for patients going to and fro to the various clinics. The whole building is very run down and in desperate need of repair, but to close the hospital would present enormous difficulties. Nonetheless, it does seem remarkable that, although built nearly two hundred years ago, it still functions as a hospital and that there is no suggestion that it should be converted to another use.

· 88 ·

THE CYCLE TRACK IN KRYLATSKOE

The decision to hold the Olympic Games in Moscow in 1980 unleashed a frenzy of building activity throughout the city in order to provide stadiums, running tracks, and swimming-pools of the required high standard. Moscow thus benefited from a great expansion of its sports facilities even though the games, boycotted by the United States and some other countries because of the Soviet invasion of Afghanistan, were not as successful as had been hoped. Among the sites throughout the city chosen for the new sports facilities and accommodation were the Olympic Village to the south-east; the football, gymnastics, skating and swimming centre on Olimpiisky Prospekt, north of the Garden Ring; and the extensive facilities developed at the new residential district of Krylatskoe, once a village which belonged to the influential Romanov boyars.

88. The Cycle Track in Krylatskoe.

Recently Krylatskoe was a place of dachas, of small country cottages on the banks of the Moskva River where the only sports were competitions in skiing, motor-cycling and motor racing. But in the mid-seventies with the Olympics in mind, it was decided to build an extensive sports complex consisting of a large rowing canal, archery facilities, a cycle-racing track and stadium. The cycle stadium was to be a covered velodrome with inclined walls for the track. It was constructed in 1976-9 by architects N. Voronin and A. Ospennikov, and is one of the most successful of modern buildings in Moscow. The track on the sloped walls has a length of 333.3 metres and the velodrome holds 6,000 spectators.

The crowning glory of this splendid edifice is the roof. Oval-shaped, it is like a large ellipse swooping down and then up again with the line of the track in perfect geometrical formation. It fits in well, too, with the nearby hill where the outdoor 13-kilometre cycle track has been built. It is refreshing to find such an outstanding and imaginative example of modern Soviet architecture so often reviled for its tendency to mimic fashions blindly from abroad.

· 89 ·

METRO PARK KULTURY

Park Kultury was the end station of the first metro line opened in 1935. It was extended to include a second line, part of the Circle, opened on 1 January 1950, in the more ornamental style of the late Stalin era. However, Park Kultury has avoided the lush decoration of some of the stations on this line in an effort to mirror the classical purity of the *Proviantsky Sklady*, the Provisions Warehouse located opposite on the Garden Ring. With fourteen lanes of constant traffic in between the effect is rather lost.

The central hall of the station was completed in late 1949 by the architect Igor Rozhin. Grey marble dominates the walls blending into the white barrel vaulted ceiling; the only pattern is provided by the

89. Metro Park Kultury: classically composed figures of the Circle Line are set against the marble background.

flooring in marble tiles. The fine classical bas-reliefs by S.M. Rabinovich between the arches leading to the platforms represent workers enjoying their leisure. They include chess-players, dancers and musicians, and readers; the pictures are more akin to Greek sculpture than Soviet life.

The name Park Kultury is misleading, for it implies that the metro station is situated near the entrance to the Gorky Park of Culture and Rest, Moscow's most famous park. To reach the park, one must cross to the other side of the Moskva River via the Krymsky Bridge, a walk of at least twenty minutes – the metro Oktyabrskaya may even be closer. The main drawback of the otherwise excellent Moscow metro system is that the stations are far apart and often some way from one's destination.

· 90 ·

THE CHURCH OF ST NICHOLAS 'V KHAMOVNIKAKH'

In 1676-82 the Settlement of Weavers (*Khamovniki*) built their church dedicated to St Nicholas. It survives today and is one of the most popular churches in Moscow. It represents well the colourful, mid-seventeenth-century style, with its wealth of red and green coloured tiles and window frames standing out vividly against the pure white background of the church walls. In a Moscow dominated by pastels and dark greys it appears like a bright child's toy or a vision out of a fairy-tale.

Inside the narrow space under the main cupola with the apse closed off by the iconostasis, is the main body of the church. The icon frame was made in the seventeenth century, but the icons themselves vary in date; the frescoes were painted in the nineteenth century. St Nicholas the Wonderworker, a kindly fourth-century bishop renowned for delivering people from mortal danger and the saint from whom Father Christmas originated, is one of the most popular saints in Russia, patron alike of sailors and farmers and weavers. In 1087 on 22 May his relics were removed to Bari in Italy and this date is regarded as his second feast-day in the Russian Church. The photograph was taken just after this festival when the lectern and altar were draped in wreaths of carnations.

90. St Nicholas: the iconostasis is decked with flowers in honour of the saint's day.

Moscow in the seventeenth century was a large city organized in *slobody* or settlements based on specialized crafts such as metalwork, armaments, various foods, icon painting, pottery and the production of tiles. Among these crafts the manufacture of textiles was one of the most highly developed requiring a large and skilled labour force. Its significance is attested to by the fact that the *sukonniki* or merchants dealing in textiles were a privileged minority near the top of Moscow society well above the townspeople. In the 1620s the weavers' settlement was formed in the western part of the city and quickly became one of the most flourishing. The settlement was organized almost like a monastic community with strict rules of conduct (children of weavers were not allowed to marry outside the settlement), and its own buildings within a defined area where only weavers and their families were allowed to reside. The central stone medieval building of the weavers where they would come daily to work on their looms still stands a few steps away from the church. The settlement system declined after the capital was moved to St Petersburg at the beginning of the eighteenth century, but textiles in the form of a silk factory built a century ago still dominate this part of Moscow and the Church of St Nicholas still stands as a testament to the erstwhile wealth of the weavers.

INDEX

Page references in italics refer to illustrations